Sensible Forex

A Common Sense Guide to Trading the World's Most Volatile Market

Sensible Forex
A Common Sense Guise to Trading
The World's Most Volatile Market
By J.J. "Jeff" Glenellis

ISBN-13: 978-1461110057
ISBN-10: 146111005X

Printed in the United States of America

Contents

Futures and Options trading has large potential rewards, but also large potential risk. You must be aware of the risks and be willing to accept them in order to invest in the futures and options markets. Don't trade with money you can't afford to lose. This is neither a solicitation nor an offer to Buy/Sell futures or options. No representation is being made that any account will or is likely to achieve profits or losses similar to those discussed on this web site. The past performance of any trading system or methodology is not necessarily indicative of future results.

*Depending upon state and country laws - always seek professional advice.

Introduction

10 years ago, had you told me I would be the author of one of the best
selling Forex books of all time, I would have said you were crazy.
Had you told me I would then go on to write a second book on the
same subject, I would have called you certifiable!

And yet, here we are.

In the two years since "Survive and Prosper" hit the bookshelves, the
one question I've fielded over and over again was "When are you
going to write another book?" My stock answer was always "I don't
know, maybe when I have something new and original to write
about." And the way things were going, the fairest way to interpret
that answer was "probably never."

But about a year ago, I began to notice something in my own trading
that I saw was lacking in so many other traders I worked with…

Confidence.

When I saw a trade setting up, I fired in an order. Dam the torpedoes,
full speed ahead and all that. Yet in my trade room and in others that I
frequented, there were plenty of traders who wanted to spend an

additional five minutes looking at longer term charts, adding that one extra indicator for confirmation, checking with the Magic 8-Ball, and whatever else it was they normally did to avoid actually placing a trade.

Or worse, after they had nothing left to check, they would finally place the trade, but only long after the entry price had come and gone, and right about the time the rest of us were exiting the trade with profit. Price would almost instantly turn around on them and they would end up a loser on the trade.

Maybe this scenario sounds a bit too familiar to you.

All it boils down to is that you lack sufficient confidence: confidence in yourself as a trader and confidence in the trading method you've chosen to use in the markets.

That's the bad news.

The good news is that unlike Patience and Discipline (two traits that are difficult to teach anyone above the age of 3), your Confidence Level can be at Zero Level right now, and be Sky High 6 weeks from now. It's simply a matter of practice and time.

A year ago I began to put together a series of tools and exercises designed to help traders build their Confidence up to a level where they became nearly-automatic traders. At the end of last year, I put those tools and exercises to the test with a group of 20 traders who volunteered for a "6 Week Bootcamp" composed of both group trading sessions and individual counseling. The starting skill levels in the group ran from absolute beginner up to experienced (5+ years) traders.

The results were nothing short of phenomenal. Traders who were at best just treading water and not seeing any gains in their accounts were now showing consistent gains on a daily and weekly basis. One trader joined after blowing up a $10,000 account, and as of today's date, has recouped 80% of that loss and has turned himself into the kind of ruthless, cold-blooded trader he knew he could be.

Even he can't describe how much confidence he has in his own trading now, other than to say that he no longer "thinks" about his trading. Once he sees a trade signal from the system he uses, he takes the trade. Yes, he has a losing trade now and then. But his losers are small, and his winners seem to run forever (his words) and that, my friends, is how you make your fortune trading Forex.

And helping you put yourself in the same or similar place is the point of this book.

If you will accept and absorb the ideas in this book, do the exercises as I describe them, and ultimately put what you learn here into action, you cannot help but become more confident in your trading and in yourself as a trader.

And the added confidence will ultimately result in your making more money as a Forex trader.

So let's get started.

Chapter 1

Using Goals as a Confidence Builder

I bet I know what you're thinking right now...

"Oh brother! Not goal setting! That shi, er, stuff never works!"

Believe me, I feel your pain. In my lifetime I've probably read more than 100 books on self-improvement, and literally every single one includes a huge section on Goal Setting. After two or three books, I would flip right past those chapters and get on with reading about the good stuff.

BIG MISTAKE!

No matter how tempting it is to skip forward to the next chapter, please don't. Just read through these next few pages and take some time to really think about what it is I'm asking you to do.

And if you don't want to listen to me on this one, listen to what one of my Inaugural Bootcamp participants had to say on the subject:

"For me, the best part of Bootcamp was the time you spent on goal setting. I had never really thought about setting an actual dollar figure as a goal, then breaking it down into those "bite-sized bits" you talked about. But once I did that, it really gave me a sense of purpose every day when I started trading, and as I started hitting my first few initial goals, the feeling of accomplishment I got was one of the best feelings I ever had while trading Forex. It even gave me something concrete to show my wife, and as she saw me making advances in my trading, she even got more supportive of my efforts, asking me what "our" goal was for the day."

What you need to remember about trading Forex is that it is an actual business you are engaging in. Sure, you don't need to rent an office or a shop, and you don't need employees or inventory, but it is a business just the same. You are devoting both time and capital in an effort to make money. That is as basic a definition of "business" as there is, and it describes your efforts in Forex down to a "t."

Now if you were to want to start a "traditional" business, such as a pizza parlor or an oil-n-lube shop, the odds are you would need to approach a bank to borrow some money to get your business off the ground. I guarantee you that before the bank even agrees to talk with you, they will want to see your business plan...you know, that thing that describes what you want to do, how you plan to do it, and how much money you plan to make doing it.

And you cannot even begin to formulate a business plan without engaging in some serious GOAL SETTING.

Sensible Forex

Are you beginning to see where I'm going with this?

You can't run a business without a business plan, and every business plan lists out in detail your short, intermediate and long term goals for said business.

You should be doing the same for your Forex business.

In "Survive and Prosper" you were given a template for the what-to-do and how-to-do-it aspects of the plan. But the financial goal setting aspect was glossed over to a great degree.

Here is where I fix that, once and for all.

Nearly every trader I ever met has this overall goal of making a million dollars trading Forex.

But that isn't really a goal. It's more of a dream.

A goal would look something like this: I am going to make $1,000,000 from my Forex trading. I am starting tomorrow with an account of $1,000, and I am going to reach my goal of $1,000,000 in 500 trading days.

Notice the difference?

Specificity.

A goal is something you have fleshed out with sufficient details to make it a real possibility for you to achieve. And in fact, as you will see shortly, the above "goal" is not even close to including the kind of details you need to make the goal "real" to you.

But it beats the heck out of "I wanna make a million dollars."

Sensible Forex

Why Are You Trading Forex?

Have you ever given that question some serious thought? If not, you're about to start.

No one I ever heard of jumped into Forex with a goal of blowing up two or three accounts and losing several thousand dollars. Yet that is exactly what most traders end up doing.

Would having a solid plan in place before they entered that first order have guaranteed them success?

No, but it would have improved their chances drastically. At least on those days where things went right, they would have had a chance to end the day winners, and carry that momentum over into their next trading session.

So why are you trading Forex?

Sure, you want to make money, but how much? In what time frame? And for what purpose?

Money is great, but as Warren Buffet and most multi-millionaires and billionaires will tell you, money is just a way to keep score. Eventually you'll want to spend some of that money on something.

So what is it you want to buy? A house? A second house? Cars? Boats? A plane? Early retirement?

It doesn't matter to me...it's your dream we're talking about here.

So go get a piece of paper (or a whole pad if you have a lot of dreams). Write down in a list everything you want to buy with your Forex earnings.

Sensible Forex

Once you have that list, write down a figure next to each item which represents how much you think it will take to buy that item. Ballpark the figure if you don't have an exact amount in mind.

Now total up all those figures.

That gives you at least a starting idea on how much you want to earn from your trading.

Now look at all those items, and add in a second figure that will cover annual taxes (real estate, personal property taxes, DMV fees, etc.) and then a third figure for the normal maintenance and upkeep on all those things you want to buy (hey, the lawn at your vacation home won't mow itself now, will it?)

Now you have a revised figure to work with.

But of course, you have daily, weekly, monthly and annual needs of your own (as does your wife, your kids, your mistress…actually, don't write that last one down. Keep that figure in your head if you value your life, or at least the other half of what you already do own).

Now total it all up.

If you come in anywhere under one million dollars, you my friend are in a very small minority. I've run this exercise with more than 100 people and to date only 3 quoted back smaller than 7 figures to me (and one of the three missed 1 mil by about five thousand dollars).

Now that you know what your dream life is going to cost, let's interject a little reality.

The odds are, you are NOT going to make a million dollars trading Forex, *at least not anytime soon.* The amount of money you would need in your trading account, combined with the size of the trades you would need to place in order to make sufficient money each day/week/month to accumulate a million bucks will ultimately scare off all but the hardiest of traders.

Don't believe me?

How do you feel when you are trading a single mini-lot ($1 pip) and see your account is down $50? Most people experience a combination of anger and nausea when they dump 50 pips on a trade.

Now imagine how that would feel if you were trading 50 full lots and your 50 pip loss was costing you $25,000?

Your local Suicide Hotline would probably add a direct line to your house to help you avoid busy signals.

My point is, most people who are trading Forex are not used to dealing with big money transactions, and at some point are going to reach a level where they simply cannot increase the size of their trade. Maybe their "wall" is at 10 lots, or 20, or even 100 lots.

But when it's your money on the line, and every tick of the chart moving in the wrong direction is costing you $500 or $1,000, you are going to need a cast iron stomach to hang in on a trade like that, and continue to place future similar sized trades.

So let's talk about realistic goal setting.

One of my Bootcampers set up an incredibly intelligent plan for himself. He currently works in a job that earns him $36,000 a year. Instead of shooting for the Million Dollar Moon, his plan is to make twice his annual salary from his trading, and once he achieves that goal consistently for two years, he plans to quit his job and be a full-

Sensible Forex

time trader (full-time being code for simply making most of his money from Forex trading…his actual trading time is usually less than 2 hours a day).

And once he does quit his job, he will have saved up approximately 2 years of his prior salary, so if/when he hits a rough patch, he has savings to fall back on.

Like I said, incredibly intelligent. And from my conversations with him, I have no doubt he will execute his plan to the fullest.

So what about you?

How much money would you need to make from trading Forex each month to really start living comfortably?

Many, many years ago I found myself being dragged to various and sundry Multi-Level Marketing presentations by well meaning friends and family. One of the themes that seemed to run through every presentation was what an extra $500 a month would mean to the average family.

Accounting for inflation, I'm guessing that figure is probably up to $1,000 by now, but the theory would be the same: an extra $1,000 a month would raise the standard of living for most families from "just getting by" to "finally getting ahead." All the bills would be paid (and on time!) and there would even be enough left over to throw into a savings account.

This may or may not apply to you. Maybe an extra thousand bucks wouldn't even begin to dig you out of your hole. Or maybe it's enough to put you right in the middle of Easy Street.

But there is a number out there that fits you like a glove. You just need to figure out what that number is.

Let's say you need an extra $3,000 a month to really be able to relax and enjoy life (that would be an extra $36,000 a year, or what most people make from a full time job, so this would be like having a clone to send out and work a full-time job and then come home each week and hand you it's paycheck).

$3,000 would be equal to 3,000 $1 pips (a single mini-lot). The odds are pretty good you aren't currently banging out 3,000 pips a month, so let's go ahead and discard that figure as unlikely.

But $3,000 would also equal 300 $10 pips (a single full lot). Now we're getting somewhere. Assuming 20 trading days a month, that would mean you would need to show 15 pips profit a day, trading a single full lot.

This is a very achievable goal.

But let's take it a bit further.

$3,000 would also equal 150 $20 pips (2 full lots). Again assuming 20 trading days a month, you would need to show 7-8 pips profit a day in order to consistently earn $3,000 a month. I can honestly say I have earned 7-8 pips on a single trade during every single hour the market is open. I've traded all three sessions in my years as a trader, and even during the "dead" hours of 3-5 p.m. eastern, you can usually pick up 7-8 pips on a trade.

That means literally EVERYONE who wants to trade Forex can do so profitably, no matter what kind of work schedule they may be forced to follow. After all, who doesn't have 1 free hour in a day to trade?

Of course, you can't expect to trade one full lot on a $100 account. If you were willing to be somewhat aggressive, you could justify trading one full lot on a $10,000 account. If you are a bit more conservative, you would want an account balance of $20,000 before you start firing in full-lot trades.

Double those numbers to trade two full lots: ($20,000 for an aggressive trader, $40,000 for a conservative trader).

Of course, here is where reality once again raises its ugly head: most traders don't start with $20,000. Or even $10,000. In fact, only 50% of the retail trading market opens an account with $1,000 or more. That means about half of you have a lot of work cut out for you if you really want to make Forex work for you.

But no one gets rich overnight trading Forex, unless they started out rich to begin with. It's simply going to take you more time to build your account. But it can be done and has been done by many people who came before you. So be confident in yourself and you will get there too.

Going back to our example, let's assume you are one of the 50% who starts out with at least $1,000. And for simple math purposes, let's assume you are aggressive enough to trade a single mini-lot ($1 pip) with that $1,000 starting balance. And finally, I'm going to assume you have sufficient trading skills to consistently bank 20 pips per day.

There are as many ways to build out this progression as there are people who are going to try. But this is the simplest one to compute, even though it will take you a little longer to reach your goal of a sufficiently funded account to start earning $3,000 a month.

Your first goal is going to be to double your account from $1,000 to $2,000. You are going to be trading one mini-lot ($1 pips) until you've reached your goal. Using the assumption listed a couple of paragraphs back (20 pips/day), your first build out would look like this:

20 pips/day x 5 trading days/week x 10 trading weeks = 1,000 pips ($1,000).

If you like your math in the form of word problems, you earn 20 pips per day, trade 5 days a week (which makes your gain 100 pips per week) and would need 10 weeks to reach your first goal of 1,000 pips (or $1,000).

Your account is now at $2,000. You can now trade $2 pips (two mini-lots). You are still shooting for 20 pips a day.

20 pips/day x 5 trading days/week x 10 trading weeks = 1,000 pips ($2,000).

After 20 trading weeks (about 5 months) you have grown your account from $1,000 to $4,000 and are fast approaching the goal of $10,000 you would need to start trading full lots. You can now trade $4 pips (four mini-lots).

20 pips/day x 5 trading days/week x 10 weeks = 1,000 pips ($4,000).

Your account is now at $8,000. You can trade $8 pips (eight mini-lots).

20 pips/day x 5 trading days/week x 3 trading week = 300 pips ($2,400).

So you trade for approximately 8 months, shooting for 20 pips a day in profit (a very reasonable and achievable goal) and increasing the size of your trade every time you double your account. In that time, you've increased your account from $1,000 to $10,400 and can now

Sensible Forex

trade a full lot ($10 pips).

As you are consistently earning 20 pips a day during this time period, you can simply keep that same daily goal and make $200 a day, pulling out your $3,000 goal each month and letting the remainder accumulate in your account to provide some extra cushion. Or you can pull out more than $3,000 a month. Or less. It's your account. You can do whatever you like with it.

The point is, you set some goals ($3,000 a month income; 20 pips a day), you reached your goals, and you profited handsomely for your efforts.

Do you still think goal setting is a useless endeavor?

Or maybe now you can see that it might just have some slight relevance to your trading life.

The idea of having a daily pip goal didn't originate with me. Plenty of traders who came before me knew the value of having something to shoot for each day they traded, and more importantly, knew the value of walking away once said goal was achieved.

Nothing hurts more than to trade for 5 minutes, hit your goal, and then decide to stick around and see if you can get a little more in one more trade. After all, it's a shame to walk away from a market that's giving away 10 or 20 pip trades on demand.

But what invariably happens is you end up giving back everything you just made plus a little extra, and instead of being up 20 on the day, you're now down 5 and you have to start looking for another trade setup just to get back to break-even.

Of course, this also puts you in a terrible frame of mind for trading, and too many traders start fudging their own rules in order to justify taking the very next trade they see. This leads to less-than-optimal trades and more losses, and before you know it, you've blown up another account.

Trust me on this one. I've been there. I know!

So set a primary goal, and then break it down into daily increments (preferably increments you know you can reach without difficulty…100 pips a day is probably too ambitious for 99.9% of the traders out there). Then trade each day until you hit that daily goal.

As long as you are consistent in your efforts, it will only be a matter of time before you end up reaching your primary goal, and it will then be time to set some new goals.

To wrap up this chapter, I am going to share some Stair Steps I created a while back, to show you how quickly one can turn a small starting amount ($1,000) into 7 figures, using a daily goal that is not at all hard to reach.

But before I do that, let me acknowledge that is **HIGHLY UNLIKELY** you or anyone else (myself included) would be successful in making 20 pips every single day as it would seem to be called for by these Stair Steps.

That is not the point.

The point of these Stair Steps is to give you some guidelines to follow as you start having winning days. As your account balance grows, you increase the size of your trade according to where your balance falls on the Stair Step you chose to follow. Should you end up down "x" pips at the end of the day, you go backwards on the Stair Step, setting the size of your next trade according to where your account balance jibes with the Stair Step.

In a way, it's like the game Candyland. You can move forward five cards in a row, and then on your next draw you get knocked back 3 spaces because your evil 5 year old niece is reshuffling the deck to ensure your next card is a loser. So when you end up in the Forex version of Molasses Swamp, you eat your losses, move backwards on the Stair Step and get ready for tomorrow's trading.

One more note about these Stair Steps…they were designed for use with a trading method called "Mrs. Watanabe's Secret" which will be described in full detail later on in this book. The Money Management aspect of these Stair Steps is hyper-aggressive simply because the Mrs. W. trading method has shown a tremendous win/loss ratio, which justified the greater risk. If you are currently using a trading method that wins 7 out of 10 times (or better) then you might consider using one of these Stair Steps as your Money Management guide.

Forex Stair-Step I

This Stair-Step assumes the following:

- A $1,000 starting account balance
- A goal of 10 pips profit for each trading session (Pip value $1/$10)

Day	Starting Balance	Trade Size	New Balance
1	1,000	.2	1,020
2	1,020	.2	1,040
3	1,040	.2	1,060
4	1,060	.2	1,080
5	1,080	.2	1,100

6	1,100	.2	1,120
7	1,120	.2	1,140
8	1,140	.2	1,160
9	1,160	.2	1,180
10	1,180	.2	1,200
11	1,200	.2	1,220
12	1,220	.2	1,240
13	1,240	.2	1,260
14	1,260	.2	1,280
15	1,280	.2	1,300
16	1,300	.2	1,320
17	1,320	.2	1,340
18	1,340	.2	1,360
19	1,360	.2	1,380
20	1,380	.2	1,400
21	1,400	.2	1,420
22	1,420	.2	1,440
23	1,440	.2	1,460
24	1,460	.2	1,480
25	1,480	.2	1,500
26	1,500	.3	1,530
27	1,530	.3	1,560
28	1,560	.3	1,590
29	1,590	.3	1,620
30	1,620	.3	1,650
31	1,650	.3	1,680
32	1,680	.3	1,710
33	1,710	.3	1,740
34	1,740	.3	1,770
35	1,770	.3	1,800
36	1,800	.3	1,830
37	1,830	.3	1,860
38	1,860	.3	1,890
39	1,890	.3	1,920

40	1,920	.3	1,950
41	1,950	.3	1,980
42	1,980	.3	2,010
43	2,010	.4	2,050
44	2,050	.4	2,090
45	2,090	.4	2,130
46	2,130	.4	2,170
47	2,170	.4	2,210
48	2,210	.4	2,250
49	2,250	.4	2,290
50	2,290	.4	2,330
51	2,330	.4	2,370
52	2,370	.4	2,410
53	2,410	.4	2,450
54	2,450	.4	2,490
55	2,490	.4	2,530
56	2,530	.5	2,580
57	2,580	.5	2,630
58	2,630	.5	2,680
59	2,680	.5	2,730
60	2,730	.5	2,780
61	2.780	.5	2,830
62	2,830	.5	2,880
63	2,880	.5	2,930
64	2,930	.5	2,980
65	2,980	.5	3,030
66	3.030	.6	3,090
67	3,090	.6	3,150
68	3,150	.6	3,210
69	3,210	.6	3,270
70	3,270	.6	3,330
71	3,330	.6	3,390
72	3,390	.6	3,450
72	3,450	.6	3,510

73	3,510	.7	3,580
74	3,580	.7	3,650
75	3,650	.7	3,720
76	3,720	.7	3,790
77	3,790	.7	3,860
78	3,860	.7	3,930
79	3,930	.7	4,000
80	4,000	.8	4,080
81	4,080	.8	4,160
82	4,160	.8	4,240
83	4,240	.8	4,320
84	4,320	.8	4,400
85	4,400	.8	4,480
86	4,480	.8	4,560
87	4,560	.9	4,650
88	4,650	.9	4,740
89	4,740	.9	4.830
90	4,830	.9	4,920
91	4,920	.9	5,010
92	5,010	1.0	5,110
93	5,110	1.0	5,210
94	5,210	1.0	5,310
95	5,310	1.0	5,410
96	5,410	1.0	5,510
97	5,510	1.1	5,620
98	5,620	1.1	5,730
99	5,730	1.1	5,840
100	5,840	1.1	5,950
101	5,950	1.1	6,060
102	6,060	1.2	6,180
103	6,180	1.2	6,300
104	6,300	1.2	6,420
105	6,420	1.2	6,540
106	6,540	1.3	6,670

Sensible Forex

107	6,670	1.3	6,800
108	6,800	1.3	6,930
109	6,930	1.3	7,060
110	7,060	1.4	7,200
111	7,200	1.4	7,340
112	7,340	1.4	7,480
113	7,480	1.4	7,620
114	7,620	1.5	7,770
115	7,770	1.5	7,920
116	7,920	1.5	8,070
117	8,070	1.6	8,230
118	8,230	1.6	8,390
119	8,390	1.6	8,550
120	8,550	1.7	8,720
121	8,720	1.7	8,890
122	8,890	1.7	9,060
123	9,060	1.8	9,240
124	9,240	1.8	9,420
125	9,420	1.8	9,600
126	9,600	1.9	9,790
127	9,790	1.9	9,980
128	9,980	1.9	10,170
129	10,170	2.0	10,370
130	10,370	2.0	10,570
131	10,570	2.1	10,780
132	10,780	2.1	10,990
133	10,990	2.1	11,200
134	11,200	2.2	11,420
135	11,420	2.2	11,640
136	11,640	2.3	11,870
137	11,870	2.3	12,130
138	12,130	2.4	12,370
139	12,370	2.4	12,610
140	12,610	2.5	12,860

141	12,860	2.5	13,110
142	13,110	2.6	13,370
143	13,370	2.6	13,530
144	13,530	2.7	13,800
145	13,800	2.7	14,070
149	14,070	2.8	14,360
150	14,360	2.8	14,640
151	14,640	2.9	14,930
152	14,930	2.9	15,220
153	15,220	3.0	15,520
154	15,520	3.1	15,830
155	15,830	3.1	16,140
156	16,140	3.2	16,460
157	16,460	3.2	16,780
158	16,780	3.3	17,110
159	17,110	3.4	17,450
160	17,450	3.4	17,790
161	17,790	3.5	18,140
162	18,140	3.6	18,500
163	18,500	3.7	18,870
164	18,870	3.7	19,240
165	19,240	3.8	19,620
166	19,620	3.9	20,010
167	20,010	4.0	20,410
168	20,410	4.0	20,810
169	20,810	4.1	21,220
170	21,220	4.2	21,630
171	21,630	4.3	22,060
172	22,060	4.4	22,500
173	22,500	4.5	22,950
174	22,950	4.5	23,400
175	23,400	4.6	23,860
176	23,860	4.7	24,330
177	24,330	4.8	24,810

178	24,810	4.9	25,300
179	25,300	5.0	25,800
180	25,800	5.1	26,310
181	26,310	5.2	26,830
182	26,820	5.3	27,360
183	27,360	5.4	27,900
184	27,900	5.5	28,450
185	28,450	5.6	29,010
186	29,010	5.8	29,590
187	29,590	5.9	30,180
188	30,180	6.0	30,780
189	30,780	6.1	31,390
190	31,390	6.2	32,010
191	32,010	6.4	32,650
192	32,650	6.5	33,300
193	33,300	6.6	33,960
194	33,960	6.7	34,630
195	34,630	6.9	35,320
196	35,320	7.0	36,020
197	36,020	7.2	36,740
198	36,740	7.3	37,470
199	37,470	7.4	38,210
200	38,210	7.6	38,970
201	38,970	7.7	39,740
202	39,740	7.9	40,530
203	40,530	8.1	41,340
204	41,340	8.2	42,160
205	42,160	8.4	43,000
206	43,000	8.6	43,860
207	43,860	8.7	44,730
208	44,730	8.9	45,620
209	45,620	9.1	46,530
210	46,530	9.3	47,460
211	47,460	9.4	48,400

212	48,400	9.6	49,360
213	49,360	9.8	50,340
214	50,340	10.0	51,340
215	51,340	10.0	52,340
216	52,340	10.0	53,340
217	53,340	10.0	54,340
218	54,340	10.0	55,340
219	55,340	11	56,440
220	56,440	11	57,540
221	57,540	11	58,640
222	58,640	11	59,740
223	59,740	11	60,840
224	60,840	12	62,040
225	62,040	12	63,240
226	63,240	12	64,440
227	64,440	12	65,640
228	65,640	13	66,940
229	66,940	13	68,240
230	68,240	13	69,540
231	65,540	13	70,840
232	70,840	14	72,240
233	72,240	14	73,640
234	73,640	14	75,040
235	75,040	15	76,540
236	76,540	15	78,040
237	78,040	15	79,540
238	79,540	15	81,040
239	81,040	16	82,640
240	82,640	16	84,240
241	84,240	16	85,640
242	85,640	17	87,340
243	87,340	17	89,040
244	89,040	17	90,740
245	90,740	18	92,540

246	92,540	18	94,340
247	94,340	18	96,240
248	96,240	19	98,140
249	98,140	19	100,040
250	100,040	20	102,040
251	102,040	20	104.040
252	104,040	20	106,040
253	106,040	21	108,140
154	108,140	21	110,240
155	110,240	22	112,440
156	112,440	22	114,640
157	114,640	22	116,840
158	116,840	23	119,140
159	119,140	23	121,440
160	121,440	24	123,840
161	123,840	24	126,240
161	126,240	25	128,740
161	128,740	25	131,240
162	131,240	26	133,840
163	133,840	26	136,440
164	136,440	27	139,140
165	139,140	27	141,840
166	141,840	28	144,640
167	144,640	28	147,440
168	147,440	29	150,340
169	150,340	30	153,340
170	153,340	30	156,340
171	156,340	31	159,440
172	159,440	31	162,540
173	162,540	32	165,740
174	165,740	33	169,040
175	169,040	33	172,340
176	172,340	34	175,740
177	175,740	35	179,240

178	179,240	35	182,740
179	182,740	36	186,340
180	186,340	37	190,040
181	190,040	38	193,840
182	193,840	38	197,640
183	197,640	39	201,540
184	201,540	40	205,540
185	205,540	41	209,640
186	209,640	41	213,740
187	213,740	42	217,940
188	217,940	43	222,240
189	222,240	44	226,640
190	226,640	45	231,140
191	231,140	46	235,740
192	235,740	47	240,440
193	240,440	48	245,240
194	245,240	49	250,140
195	250,140	50	255,140
196	255,140	51	260,240
197	260,240	52	265,440
198	265,440	53	270,740
199	270,740	54	276,140
200	276,140	55	281,640
201	281,640	56	287,240
202	287,240	57	292,940
203	292,940	58	298,740
204	298,740	59	304,640
205	304,640	60	310,640
206	310,640	62	316,840
207	316,840	63	323,140
208	323,140	64	329,540
209	329,540	65	336,040
210	336,040	67	342,740
211	342,740	68	349,540

212	349,540	69	356,440
213	356,440	71	363,540
214	363,540	72	370,740
215	370,740	74	378,140
216	378,140	75	385,640
217	385,640	77	393,340
218	393,340	78	401,140
219	401,140	80	409,140
220	409,140	81	417,240
221	417,240	83	425,540
222	425,540	85	434,040
223	434,040	86	442,640
224	442,640	88	451,440
225	451,440	90	460,440
226	460,440	92	469,640
227	469,640	93	478,940
228	478,940	95	488,440
229	488,440	97	498,140
230	498,140	99	508,040
231	508,040	100	518,040
232	518,040	100	528,040
233	528,040	100	538,040
234	538,040	100	548,040
235	548,040	100	558,040
236	558,040	100	568,040
237	568,040	100	578,040
238	578,040	100	588,040
239	588,040	100	598,040
240	598,040	100	608,040
241	608,040	100	618,040
242	618,040	100	628,040
243	628,040	100	638,040
244	638,040	100	648,040
245	648,040	100	658,040

246	658,040	100	668,040
247	668,040	100	678,040
248	678,040	100	688,040
249	688,040	100	698,040
250	698,040	100	708,040
251	708,040	100	718,040
252	718,040	100	728,040
253	728,040	100	738,040
254	738,040	100	748,040
255	748,040	100	758,040
256	758,040	100	768,040
257	768,040	100	778,040
258	778,040	100	788,040
259	788,040	100	798,040
260	798,040	100	808,040
261	808,040	100	818,040
262	818,040	100	828,040
263	828,040	100	838,040
264	838,040	100	848,040
265	848,040	100	858,040
266	858,040	100	868,040
267	868,040	100	878,040
268	878,040	100	888,040
269	888,040	100	898,040
270	898,040	100	908,040
271	908,040	100	918,040
272	918,040	100	928,040
273	928,040	100	938,040
274	938,040	100	948,040
275	948,040	100	958,040
276	958,040	100	968,040
277	968,040	100	978,040
278	978,040	100	988,040
279	988,040	100	998,040

280	998,040	100	1,008,040

This Stair Step ceases the Lot Progression at 100 full lots due to most brokers having a rule in place that guarantees "instant fills" up to 100 lots. Beyond 100 lots and you could run into liquidity issues with your broker. You are free to continue the Lot Progression beyond 100 lots if you so desire.

Forex Stair-Step II

This Stair-Step assumes the following:

- A $1,000 starting account balance
- A goal of 20 pips profit for each trading session (Pip value $1/$10)

Day	Starting Balance	Trade Size	New Balance
1	1,000	.2	1,040
2	1,040	.2	1,080
3	1,080	.2	1,120
4	1,120	.2	1,160
5	1,160	.2	1,200
6	1,200	.2	1,240
7	1,240	.2	1,280
8	1,280	.2	1,320
9	1,320	.2	1,360
10	1,360	.2	1,400
11	1,400	.2	1,440
12	1,440	.2	1,480
13	1,480	.2	1,520
14	1,520	.3	1,580
15	1,580	.3	1,640

Sensible Forex

16	1,640	.3	1,700
17	1,700	.3	1,760
18	1,760	.3	1,820
19	1,820	.3	1,880
20	1,880	.3	1,940
21	1,940	.3	2,000
22	2,000	.4	2,080
23	2,080	.4	2,160
24	2,160	.4	2,240
25	2,240	.4	2,320
26	2,320	.4	2,400
27	2,400	.4	2,480
28	2,480	.4	2,560
29	2,560	.5	2,660
30	2,660	.5	2,760
31	2,760	.5	2,860
32	2,860	.5	2,960
33	2,960	.5	3,060
34	3,060	.6	3,180
35	3,180	.6	3,300
36	3,300	.6	3,420
37	3,420	.6	3,540
38	3,540	.7	3,680
39	3,680	.7	3,820
40	3,820	.7	3,960
41	3,960	.7	4,100
42	4,100	.8	4,260
43	4,260	.8	4,420
44	4,420	.8	4,580
45	4,580	.9	4,760
46	4,760	.9	4,940
47	4,940	.9	5,120
48	5,120	1.0	5,320
49	5,320	1.0	5,520

50	5,520	1.1	5,740
51	5,740	1.1	5,960
52	5,960	1.1	6,180
53	6,180	1.2	6,420
54	6,420	1.2	6,660
55	6,660	1.3	6,920
56	6,920	1.3	7,180
57	7,180	1.4	7,460
58	7,460	1.4	7,740
59	7,740	1.5	8,040
60	8,040	1.6	8,360
61	8,360	1.6	8,680
62	8,680	1.7	9,020
63	9.020	1.8	9,380
64	9,380	1.8	9,740
65	9,740	1.9	10,120
66	10,120	2.0	10,520
67	10,520	2.1	10,940
68	10,940	2.1	11,360
69	11,360	2.2	11,800
70	11,800	2.3	12,260
71	12,260	2.4	12,740
72	12,740	2.5	13,240
73	13,240	2.6	13,760
74	13,760	2.7	14,300
75	14,300	2.8	14,860
76	14,860	2.9	15,440
77	15,440	3.0	16,040
78	16,040	3.2	16,680
79	16,680	3.3	17,340
80	17,340	3.4	18,020
81	18,020	3.6	18,740
82	18,740	3.7	19,480
83	19,480	3.8	20,240

84	20,240	4.0	21,040
85	21,040	4.2	21,880
86	21,880	4.3	22,740
87	22,740	4.5	23,640
88	23,640	4.7	24,580
89	24,580	4.9	25,560
90	25,560	5.1	26,580
91	26,580	5.3	27,640
92	27,640	5.5	28,740
93	28,740	5.7	29,880
94	29,880	5.9	31,060
95	31,060	6.2	32,300
96	32,300	6.4	33,580
97	33,580	6.7	34,920
98	34,920	6.9	36,300
99	36,300	7.2	37,740
100	37,740	7.5	39,240
101	39,240	7.8	40,800
102	40,800	8.1	42,420
103	42.420	8.4	44,100
104	44,100	8.8	45,860
105	45,860	9.1	47,680
106	47,680	9.5	49,580
107	49,580	9.9	51,560
108	51,560	10.0	53,560
109	53,560	10.0	55,560
110	55,560	11.0	57,760
111	57,760	11.0	59.960
112	59,960	11.0	62,160
113	62,150	12.0	64,560
114	64,560	12.0	66,960
115	66,960	13.0	69,560
116	69,560	13.0	72,160
117	72,160	14.0	74,960

118	74,960	14.0	77,740
119	77,740	15.0	80,740
120	80,740	16.0	83,940
121	83,940	16.0	87,140
122	87,140	17.0	90,540
123	90,540	18.0	94,140
124	94,140	18.0	97,740
125	97,740	19.0	101,540
126	101,540	20.0	105,540
127	105,540	21.0	109,740
128	109,740	21.0	113,940
129	113,940	22.0	118,340
130	118,340	23.0	122,940
131	122,940	24.0	127,740
132	127,740	25.0	132,740
133	132,740	26.0	137,940
134	137,940	27.0	143,340
135	143,340	28.0	148,940
136	148,940	29.0	154,740
137	154,740	30.0	160,740
138	160,740	32.0	167,140
139	167,140	33.0	173,740
140	173,740	34.0	182,540
141	182,540	36.0	189,740
142	189,740	37.0	197,400
143	197,400	39.0	205,200
144	205,200	41.0	213,400
145	213,400	42.0	221,800
146	221,800	44.0	230,600
147	230,600	46.0	239,800
148	239,800	47.0	249,400
149	249,400	49.0	259,200
150	259,200	51.0	269,400
151	269,400	53.0	280,000

152	280,000	56.0	291,200
153	291,200	58.0	302,800
154	302,800	60.0	314,800
155	314,800	62.0	327,200
156	327,200	65.0	340,200
157	340,200	68.0	353,800
158	353,800	70.0	367,800
159	367,800	73.0	382,400
160	382,400	76.0	397,600
161	397,600	79.0	413,800
162	413,800	82.0	430,200
163	430,200	86.0	447,400
164	447,200	89.0	465,200
165	465,200	93.0	483,800
166	483,800	96.0	503,000
167	503,000	100.0	523,000
168	523,000	100.0	543,000
169	543,000	100.0	563,000
170	563,000	100.0	583,000
171	583,000	100.0	603,000
172	603,000	100.0	623,000
173	623,000	100.0	643,000
174	643,000	100.0	663,000
175	663,000	100.0	683,000
176	683,000	100.0	703,000
177	703,000	100.0	723,000
178	723,000	100.0	743,000
179	743,000	100.0	763,000
180	763,000	100.0	783,000
181	783,000	100.0	803,000
182	803,000	100.0	823,000
183	823,000	100.0	843,000
184	843,000	100.0	863,000
185	863,000	100.0	883,000

186	883,000	100.0	903,000
187	903,000	100.0	923,000
188	923,000	100.0	943,000
189	943,000	100.0	963,000
190	963,000	100.0	983,000
191	983,000	100.0	1,003,000

Assuming 22 trading days a month, it would take between 8 and 9 months to turn a $1,000 account into 7 figures (also assuming you traded each day until you reached your 20 pip goal, and further assuming there were no substantial breaks taken, such as Thanksgiving, Christmas/New Year and the month of August, all of which are generally considered to be poor times to trade).

Factoring in those times of poor trading (plus about a dozen or so national holidays when banks are closed and trading volume is between low and non-existent) following this 20 Pip Stair Step Method would take the average trader around 1 year to reach 7 figures, assuming a starting balance of $1,000.

Forex Stair Step III

Stair-Step Method of Increasing Forex Profits as Account Grows

Assumes:
   1. **$1,000 starting account balance**
   2. **40 pip daily target (pip value = $1/$10)**

Day	Balance	Trade Size	New Balance
1	1,000	.2	1,080
2	1,080	.2	1,160

3	1,160	.2	1,240
4	1,240	.2	1,320
5	1,320	.2	1,400
6	1,400	.2	1,480
7	1,480	.2	1,560
8	1,560	.3	1,680
9	1,680	.3	1,800
10	1,800	.3	1,920
11	1,920	.3	2,040
12	2,040	.4	2,200
13	2,200	.4	2,360
14	2,360	.4	2,500
15	2,500	.5	2,700
16	2,700	.5	2,900
17	2,900	.5	3,100
18	3,100	.6	3,340
19	3,340	.6	3,580
20	3,580	.7	3,860
21	3,860	.7	4,140
22	4,140	.8	4,460
23	4,460	.8	4,780
24	4,780	.9	5,140
25	5,140	1.0	5,540
26	5,540	1.1	5,980
27	5,980	1.1	6,420
28	6,420	1.2	6,900
29	6,900	1.3	7,420
30	7,420	1.4	7,980
31	7,980	1.5	8,580
32	8,590	1.7	9,260
33	9,260	1.8	9,980
34	9,980	1.9	10,740
35	10,740	2.1	11,580
36	11,580	2.3	12,500

37	12,500	2.5	13,500
38	13,500	2.7	14,580
39	14,580	2.9	15,740
40	15,740	3.1	16,980
41	16,980	3.3	18,320
42	18,320	3.6	19,760
43	19,760	3.9	21,320
44	21,320	4.2	23,000
45	23,000	4.6	24,840
46	24,840	4.9	26,800
47	26,800	5.0	28,800
48	28,800	5.0	30,800
49	30,800	6.0	33,200
50	33,200	6.0	35,600
51	35,600	7.0	38,400
52	38,400	7.0	41,200
53	41,200	8.0	44,400
54	44,400	8.0	47,600
55	47,600	9.0	51,200
56	51,200	10.0	55,200
57	55,200	11.0	59,600
58	59,600	11.0	64,000
59	64,000	12.0	68,800
60	68,800	13.0	74,000
61	74,000	14.0	78,800
62	78,800	15.0	84,800
63	84,800	16.0	91,200
64	91,200	18.0	98,400
65	98,400	19.0	106,000
66	106,000	21.0	114,400
67	114,400	22.0	123,200
68	123,200	24.0	132,800
69	132,800	26.0	143,200
70	143,200	28.0	154,400

71	154,400	30.0	166,400
72	166,400	33.0	179,600
73	179,600	35.0	193,600
74	193,600	38.0	208,800
75	208,800	41.0	225,200
76	225,200	45.0	243,200
77	243,200	48.0	262,200
78	262,200	52.0	283,200
79	283,200	56.0	305,600
80	305,600	61.0	330,000
81	330,000	66.0	356,400
82	356,400	71.0	384,800
83	384,800	76.0	415,200
84	415,200	83.0	448,400
85	448,400	89.0	484,000
86	484,000	96.0	522,800
87	522,800	100.0	562,800
88	562,800	100.0	602,800
89	602,800	100.0	642,800
90	642,800	100.0	682,800
91	682,800	100.0	722,800
92	722,800	100.0	762,800
93	762,800	100.0	802,800
94	802,800	100.0	842,800
95	842,800	100.0	882,800
96	882,800	100.0	922,800
97	922,800	100.0	962,800
98	962,800	100.0	1,002,800

Assuming 22 trading days a month, you could reach $1 Million in as little as 4-1/2 months.

Chapter Two

JUSTIFYING YOUR EVERY TRADING MOVE

When talking about the relationship between trader confidence and trader success, you find yourself in something of a 'chicken vs. egg" argument:

Are you a Confident Trader because you are experiencing Success, or are you experiencing Success because you are a Confident Trader?

Arguments could be made for both sides, but rather than waste time analyzing which comes first, time is much better spent working on both aspects of trading.

As noted earlier, when we are discussing Trader Confidence, we are actually looking at two different aspects: Confidence in yourself as a Trader, and Confidence in the trading system (or method) you use when trading the Forex markets.

Since it's impossible for me to know what trading system you use (assuming you use one in the first place) I'm forced to rely upon your own evaluation of the system as being meritorious enough to justify your faith.

So I'm going into this chapter assuming you have a trading method that is at least profitable 51% of the time, and preferably more. And yes, there are traders who make tons of money each year with methods that only win three out of ten trades, but then, there is a very good reason those traders probably aren't reading this book.

They don't need to.

You do.

And that's why I strongly urge you to use a trading method that wins more often than it loses. If you don't have one of those at your fingertips, or you have doubts that your current trading system will live up to the goal of more winners than losers, look in the Appendix (later, not now) for a discussion of several different methods that have proven to be profitable over time.

Confidence in your trading system is something that you gain over a period of time, simply by placing trades according to the rules of that system. The problem most traders have is that they learn about a new system, try it for a few days (usually with some degree of success) but once they have a losing day with the system, they automatically decide the system 'does not work" and they are off in search of that next winning system.

Sensible Forex

Long time traders call that the "Search for the Holy Grail" and it is a source, if not THE source, of most trader problems.

There are Two Rules about using trading systems you need to accept as Gospel:

1. There IS no such thing as a Holy Grail trading system. I don't care what you read on a sales page, or in a Forum post somewhere. It simply DOES NOT EXIST!
2. ALL trading systems and methods will run into bad streaks at some point. The key to surviving those bad streaks is to recognize them early on, and reduce your trade size until such time as the system works itself back around to being profitable.

If a trading system wins 8 out of 10 trades, that means it LOSES 2 out of 10 trades. And that DOES NOT MEAN after you lose two trades, you are automatically going to win the next eight. It merely represents some long term averages. I've used systems that racked up 10-12 losing trades in a row. When that happened, I backed off of my trading until I identified WHY I was losing, and waited until market conditions turned around and my method once again became profitable.

What I DIDN'T DO was abandon the system and go off in search of some other method that allegedly won 9 out of 10 trades. Yet that is exactly what so many newer traders do. Give them a bad day or two with a system, and they consign it to a dusty shelf on their hard drive, never to be seen (or used) again.

So Step One in becoming a Confident Trader is to find a trading system that suits your personality and style, and stick with it.

Step Two of becoming a Confident Trader is actually a corollary to

Sensible Forex

Step One. Step Two is to simply make certain you are following the rules of your Trading System down to the letter.

Now that may seem more than obvious to most of you, but hear me out.

The BIGGEST SOURCE of trader grief is losing a trade because the trader decided to "anticipate" the trade signal and get into the trade before all the rules and conditions were met. If they are using a trade system that involves three indicators, and two indicators are giving a signal while the third is lagging behind, they ignore that third indicator and jump into the trade.

"2 out of 3 Ain't Bad" is a great song by Meatloaf, but a crappy way to trade Forex. And the biggest danger is that you will win just enough of those trades to keep you in the mindset of ignoring your own system rules and jumping into trades too early. But the end result is you end up losing more and more money as a trader, simply because you aren't following the rules.

And the irony of the situation is that you blame the SYSTEM for the losses instead of *the person who is misusing* the system.

Look at it from another perspective: when NASA launches the Space Shuttle, they have a group of people monitoring the various aspects of the launch, and every single one of those Monitors must give a "thumbs up" before the Flight Director will authorize the actual launch.

How disastrous would it be if 8 out of 10 monitors gave the go-ahead, but Fuel and Electrical Systems both said "don't do this" and Flight still gave the go-ahead for launch.

We'd be experiencing a national tragedy at almost every launch.

Sensible Forex

So think of your trading as a NASA launch, and your indicators as your Systems Monitors. As long as everyone is in agreement, you launch your trade. But if any one of your Monitors is telling you to wait, you wait until that last Monitor gives you a green light, and then you enter the trade.

Yes, you will miss out on some winning trades (or at least get in later than you could have by cheating).

But you will also miss out on plenty of LOSING TRADES, when the one lagging indicator (monitor) is eventually proven to be right, and your other indicators reverse as price moves against your prospective trade.

The end result of being absolutely faithful to the rules of your trading system will be fewer losing trades, which can only mean a higher percentage of winning trades. And more winning trades can only help boost your Confidence, in both yourself and your trading system.

Now I readily admit that it is one thing to say you need to follow your own rules, and something entirely different to actually follow that advice. Everyone possesses different levels of Patience and Discipline, and those who don't have a lot of either find it extraordinarily difficult to sit on their hands and wait for the perfect signals.

If you happen to be one of those who has to constantly fight with yourself to keep from getting into less-than-optimal trades within 5 minutes of turning on your PC, then this next section is just what you need.

One of the tools I put together last year is what I call the Trade Justification Form.

Sensible Forex

I decided to create this form after having countless conversations with traders who acknowledged that they needed to keep a trading journal to document their bad trades, but just didn't have the discipline to sit down and write out their thoughts after every trade.

This form is designed to be a substitute for keeping track of your trading in journal form.

As you will see, it is set up to be answered in both Yes/No form, as well as a couple of lines where you will need to explain why you broke one of the Primary Rules of Trading.

But the genius of this form (if I may be so arrogant as to use the word "genius" to describe something I myself created) is that instead of just filling out the form for a bad trade and moving on, I strongly recommend you get someone you know and respect (a spouse, a relative, a friend, another trader) who will agree to review this form for you at least once a week, but preferably more often, and who will hold you accountable for each 'mistake" you make in your trading.

In my case, when I was developing the TJF, I got my wife to sit down and review each one of my losing trades (there weren't a lot of them by this point, but there were enough that it was highly enlightening).

Let me also add at this point that while I love my wife, the overriding emotional dynamic at work here was fear. I am absolutely terrified of her, and the last thing I really wanted to do was put myself in a position where she would be raging at me constantly for my screw-ups.

So I had a prime motivator in place to insure that the TJF worked its magic on my behalf.

Sensible Forex

I put together 2 weeks worth of forms, then sat down with her and asked her to review what I had written about my losing trades. I had already reviewed the forms in one sitting and spotted the one bad habit that kept popping up, but I wanted her to do her own review and then give me her input.

Her review was the same as mine...on almost every one of the losing trades (there were 14 total in 2 weeks) the same problem was highlighted: I was jumping in ahead of time into the trades and not waiting for ALL of my indicators to give me the same signal.

And her input was pretty much what I expected:

"How big of an idiot are you, anyway?" And it got worse from there. She put special emphasis on the fact that here I was, this "big time Forex writer and trader" who was making the same bush-league mistake, over and over again.

Like I said, it was pretty much what I expected.

Of course, she was more than happy to "volunteer" to keep reading my future TJF's to help keep me motivated to stay out of less than optimal trading situations.

And that fear of having my wife go ballistic on me and call me a moron (among other names) helped keep me focused on only trading when my system gave me the "all systems are GO!" signal.

Over the next 4 weeks, I found I was filling out fewer and fewer TJF's. In fact, during Week 3 of this experiment, I took 11 trades and every one was a winner. And as we reached the end of the 30 days, my losers all shared the same trait: I followed my trading system down to the letter but still ended up losing the trade.

File that under %&!# Happens.

The good news was that not only were there only a handful of losers at the end (3 in my last week) but instead of hanging onto the trade and trying to wait it out in the hopes it would turn around, I got out with a very small loss each time (holding on too long and moving my stop loss further and further away from my entry point was another habit I used to have, although it wasn't anywhere near as severe as my problem with early entries).

Any one of my winning trades more than covered the losses from all 3 trades combined.

I was already a good trader when I put this form together.

But thanks to the TJF, now I am a very good trader, with a much improved attitude of Discipline, and Confidence in my trading that is off the charts!

Losing trades are now meaningless to me, as I tend to jettison them long before they start costing me any real money. And since they are now fewer and farther in between, I actually welcome them, just as a reminder that I am not 10 Feet Tall and Bulletproof. That "I Cannot Lose" attitude is the worst frame of mind a trader can have, because you then feel like you can just flip a coin to find a trade and make instant profit.

That road leads one way and one way only: straight to Disaster.

It's good to have just enough losers thrown into the mix to keep you humble. Learn to celebrate those just as you do your winners.

Now that you've heard all about the TJF, let's take a look at it (and don't worry about having to copy it out of this book; in the Appendix

I give you the link where you can download an original and take it to a copy shop and have copies made).

But one last comment before we get to the form itself: You only need to fill out the TJF for your losing trades. After all, what is there to learn from your winners? You got a signal, you took the trade, you won some pips. Great.

But your losers?

Your losers can provide you a wealth of information you might not otherwise recognize without using the TJF.

So skip your winners and focus on the losers, and within the next 30 days, you should find yourself only filling out the last section of the form (and that only 2-3 times a week if you're taking this seriously!)

TRADE JUSTIFICATION FORM

Date:_____ Time:_____ Pair Traded:_____

Buy / Sell Price Entered:_____ Price Exited:_____

Profit Target:_____ Stop Loss:_____

Did You Take This Trade During a Period of High Volume (London/NY Session) Y N

If No, Why Did You Decide to Take the Trade:_____

_____

_____

Sensible Forex

Did You Use a Fixed Stop Loss: Y   N

If No, Why Not:_____

_____

If You Exited Manually and/or Prior to Hitting Your Stop Loss, Why Did You Exit Then:

_____

_____

_____

Did You Move Your Stop Loss Further Away From Your Original Price?   Y   N

Why Did You Do That?_____

_____

How Much More Did You Lose (in Pips and in Dollars) By Moving Your Stop Loss?

_____

How Many Times in This Trade Did You Move Your Stop Loss?

_____

How Many Times This Week (Covering All The Trades You Took)? _____

Is "Increasing" Your Stop Loss Regularly Working In Your Behalf?   Y   N

If "No" Then Why Do You Keep Increasing Your Stop Loss? _____

_____

Sensible Forex

Method/System Used:_____

Indicators Used:_____

Did All Indicators Support Trade at the Time It Was Placed: Y   N

If No, Then Why Did You Take The Trade:_____

_____

_____

Did You Enter The Trade On the Same Candle That Gave Out The Signal?   Y   N

If "No" Then How Many Candles Later Did You Enter the Trade? _____

Why Did You Wait So Long to Enter After You Got Your Signal? _____

_____

_____

Did a Spike in Price Hurt Your Trade   Y   N

Was There a Scheduled News Event at the Time of the Spike: Y   N

Which News Event:_____

Were You Aware This Event Was Scheduled: Y   N

If Yes, Why Did You Take and/or Remain in the Trade:_____

_____

_____

If "No" Why Were You Not Aware of the Scheduled News Event? _____

Sensible Forex

Was Price Trading in a Tight Range at the Time of Your Trade: Y   N

What Was the Range (in Pips):_____

Did You Notice the Existence of the Range Prior to Trading: Y   N

If Yes, Why Did You Take the Trade:_____

_____

If No, What Kept You From Noticing the Range:_____

_____

_____

Was the Price Trending at the Time of Your Trade: Y   N

If Yes, Was Your Trade in the Direction of the Trend: Y   N

If No to the Last Question, Why Did You Trade Against the Trend:_____

_____

_____

Did You Lose The Trade Prior to This One?   Y   N

If "Yes" Do You Think You Were In a "Revenge-Trade" Mindset?   Y   N

If "Yes" What Do You See That You Did Wrong? _____

_____

_____

If "No", Explain Why You Took This Trade: _____

If You Believe You Did Everything Right, But Still Lost, Why Do You Think You Lost?:

_____

_____

_____

While I think the TJF is pretty self-explanatory, I still want to go over the major themes involved just to make sure you understand why each section is so important.

Details of the Trade

Date:_____ Time:_____ Pair Traded:_____

Buy / Sell   Price Entered:_____ Price Exited:_____

Time Frame: _____Profit Target:_____ Stop Loss:_____

This is simply to help you identify the trade and keep the details fresh in your mind. After a week's worth of trading, all the trades kind of run together into a big pile of mush, at least for me. By keeping track of the specific details, you (and the person who is holding you accountable for each trade) can pull up the charts and see exactly what you were looking at when you took the trade.

Sensible Forex

Expected Trading Volume

Did You Take This Trade During a Period of High Volume (London/NY Session) Y
N

If No, Why Did You Decide to Take the Trade:_____

_____

_____

There is nothing wrong with trading outside of the London and/or New York sessions, but volume during the Asian session (and the "dead zone" between the close of New York and the open in Australia) is normally much lighter, and there are usually fewer truly good trading opportunities outside of the High Volume sessions.

Stop Losses

Did You Use a Fixed Stop Loss: Y   N

If No, Why Not:_____

_____

_____

If You Exited Manually and/or Prior to Hitting Your Stop Loss, Why Did You Exit Then:

_____

_____

_____

Sensible Forex

Did You Move Your Stop Loss Further Away From Your Original Price? Y   N

Why Did You Do That?_____

_____

How Much More Did You Lose (in Pips and in Dollars) By Moving Your Stop Loss?

_____

How Many Times Today Did You Move Your Stop Loss and Increase Your Exposure?

_____

How Many Times This Week (Covering All The Trades You Took)? _____

Is "Increasing" Your Stop Loss Regularly Working In Your Behalf? Y   N

If "No" Then Why Do You Keep Increasing Your Stop Loss? _____

_____

_____

The use of stop-losses cause considerable headaches for most traders, both new and experienced. Setting a stop-loss too close to your entry price gets you taken out before the trade ever has a chance to develop; moving a stop-loss farther and farther away from your entry in the vain hope that price will ultimately turn around and move in your favor is equally devastating to account balances.

If you find yourself being taken out of too many trades too early, you need to start using a larger stop loss initially. If you find yourself exposing yourself to greater losses simply because you don't want to have your initial stop triggered, you need to simply quit doing that unless you have a very sound reason, based on identifiable changing market circumstances (and the mere fact that the trade is moving against you does not qualify as one of the changing circumstances).

The Rules of Your System

Method/System Used:_____

Indicators Used:_____

Did All Indicators Support Trade at the Time It Was Placed: Y   N

If No, Then Why Did You Take The Trade:_____

_____

_____

Did You Enter The Trade On the Same Candle That Gave Out The Signal?   Y   N

If "No" Then How Many Candles Later Did You Enter the Trade? _____

Why Did You Wait So Long to Enter After You Got Your Signal? _____

_____

_____

Your system has rules…follow the rules. This was discussed in great detail a few pages back. But there is an equally troubling habit traders have when trading a specific system. They don't have enough faith in their chosen method, so when a real signal is given out, they delay their entry for one or more candles before deciding to get into the trade. Your system is either giving out signals or it is not. If it's not, you don't trade. If it is, you enter a trade immediately. Waiting 5 minutes will only cost you money in the long run.

Accounting for the News

Did a Spike in Price Hurt Your Trade   Y   N

Was There a Scheduled News Event at the Time of the Spike: Y   N

Which News Event:_____

Were You Aware This Event Was Scheduled: Y   N

If Yes, Why Did You Take and/or Remain in the Trade:_____

_____

_____

If "No" Why Were You Not Aware of the Scheduled News Event? _____

_____

_____

I've lost track of how many newer traders blame spikes in price on shady brokers who are stop-hunting their ten cent trades. 95% of the time, the spike they are blaming on the brokers is actually tied into some economic news release that caused a market reaction of some sort. Knowing when those reports are scheduled for release will save you a mountain of heartache (checking the calendar at Forex Factory each day before you place your first trade is a habit EVERY trader should get into). This section will help you get into that habit.

Range Trading

Was Price Trading in a Tight Range at the Time of Your Trade: Y   N

Sensible Forex

What Was the Range (in Pips):_____

Did You Notice the Existence of the Range Prior to Trading: Y   N

If Yes, Why Did You Take the Trade:_____

_____

If No, What Kept You From Noticing the Range:_____

_____

_____

I admit I've always had a certain blindness when it came to spotting those tight ranges that always cause Buy signals to be triggered at the top of the range, and Sell signals at the bottom. I used to need two or three bad trades in a row before I figured out I was in a range, and would back off until there was a breakout of some type. But this has forced me to do a deeper evaluation of trading conditions at the time the signal is given, and I now happily sit on my hands until price exits the range (or I start selling at the Top and Buying at the bottom, to increase me chances of actually carving out a winning trade in what are otherwise untradeable conditions).

Trend Trading

Was the Price Trending at the Time of Your Trade: Y   N

If Yes, Was Your Trade in the Direction of the Trend: Y   N

If No to the Last Question, Why Did You Trade Against the Trend:_____

_____

_____

If you are constantly trading against an existing trend, you should probably give serious thought to quitting that. Yes, some people are very successful as counter-trend traders. But it's so easy to find entries that just "go with the flow" of the trend, why would you want to risk your money by swimming against the tide?

Revenge Trading

Did You Lose The Trade Prior to This One?   Y   N

If "Yes" Do You Think You Were In a "Revenge-Trade" Mindset?   Y   N

If "Yes" What Do You See That You Did Wrong? _____

_____

_____

If "No", Explain Why You Took This Trade: _____

_____

_____

More accounts are blown to pieces by Revenge trading than by all the other bad habits combined. You get a signal (or more likely, you get 75% of a signal) and you place a trade. You lose. You get another signal (or part). You trade. You lose.

Do this 3 or 4 times in a row and you start getting a little pissed off. Or maybe a lot pissed off.

So you double the size of your trade. Or you get the next signal and trade in the opposite direction. Or you just let the Magic 8-Ball do all your thinking for you.

But by all that is Holy, you are going to get ALL your money back on this next trade.

Which you then lose.

And now you are what poker players call On Tilt. You throw caution, logic and reason to the wind and turn your platform into a mini-Las Vegas casino, and like Las Vegas, you end up losing all your money.

And you don't even get a free drink for your efforts.

Recognizing when you are starting to revenge trade (and walking away from your PC until you calm down) is one of the best skills a trader can possess. Ignoring your tendency to go 'on tilt" will ultimately be fatal to your account balance.

Just One of Those Things

If You Believe You Did Everything Right, But Still Lost, Why Do You Think You Lost?:

_____

_____

_____

You're going to lose trades now and then, no matter who you are or how good a trader you might be. The idea, though, is to limit your losers to those times when you do everything else right and still lose. Because as long as you are using a decent trading system, and following the rules of that system down to the letter, you will ultimately be winning a lot more trades than you lose.

And honestly, filling in the above section with "I have no earthly idea why I lost this one" is an acceptable answer, as long as you've looked at all the other factors involved in the trade (met your system's requirements 100%, no news releases were scheduled, etc.) and determined you had no reason to not take the trade.

Just to recap, when you use this form be brutally honest in every one of your answers. Lying to yourself (and the person who is trying to help you) is not going to do you any good. Take the criticism offered in the spirit in which it is intended (to make you the best trader you can be!) and above all, **LEARN FROM YOUR MISTAKES!** It won't do you any good to identify weaknesses in your trading if you don't make a concerted effort to eliminate those weaknesses.

But I promise you this: use this form for the next 30 days and a month from now you are going to see a radical improvement in your trading (and in your account balance).

Chapter Three

DROP BACK TEN AND PUNT

In the previous chapter's discussion of the TJF, there was some brief discussion of Revenge Trading, and how detrimental it can be to your account balance (not to mention your Confidence).

In this chapter, we're going to delve into the topic a lot deeper, and give you a couple of tools you can use to limit the damage when you suffer a meltdown (and unless you're some Forex Trading Automaton from Outer Space, you're going to have the occasional meltdown) and how to quickly recover both your Confidence and your account balance.

At some point in their trading lives, almost every Forex trader finds themselves in the very frustrating position of trading in a Loss Spiral. Simply put, a Loss Spiral is a time when everything was going along smoothly, then the trader experienced a setback (99.99% of the time it was just a losing trade). Then another loss popped up, followed by another, and then another.

At some point in this downward spiral, the trader will start experiencing doubt as to their own trading skills (no matter how much experience they might have) and also begin to place all of their focus on how much money they've lost.

And once you start worrying about the money, that's when things really get bleak.

Maybe during the course of one of these sessions you dump 10-20% of your account. Believe me, if that's all you're looking at as a loss, you're in great shape. Because most traders will go way past 20% losses, and end one of these sessions from hell with losses far in excess of 50%.

They decide they since they lost it all in one session, they're going to get it all back in one session, so they double (or triple) up on the size of their trades, figuring they only need a half or even a third as many pips as they've blown to get back to break even.

But needless to say, in their altered state of consciousness, they aren't going to find a winning trade. Instead, they bank one more loss, only this time for 2 or 3 times the amount they lost previously. And now their account balance is so low, they can barely afford to place a reasonably sized trade, much less one that throws caution to the wind.

If this sounds like I might have some personal experience in this arena, I do. The first time I blew up my account, I did so in a spectacular (and quick) showing of ignorance and stubbornness. The day started out like any other, and I even won my first trade for the day.

But my second trade was spiked out at a loss based on a scheduled news release I was not aware of (and I wasn't aware of it because I failed to check the calendar that day).

I was really pissed off by this, mostly at myself for not doing something as simple as taking 30 seconds out of my busy schedule to glance at a friggin' calendar.

But I was now down for the day, and not in a particularly good mood. My next trade was another loser (just bad luck on that one—I did everything right as far as I could tell), and I was starting to mutter to myself under my breath. I knocked out another loser when I watched +12 turn into -20, holding on too long to the trade in the hopes that it would run far enough to help me get back close to even.

Now my dogs are cowering under the bed because they've seen this side of me before (and it ain't pretty!). The next signal I got I decided play a little mind game on the market, and trade in the opposite direction (since my earlier trades following the system were losing).

Of course, this trade does exactly what it was supposed to, and I ended up dumping another 25 pips on the trade (25 pips I would have banked had I not tried to outsmart those invisible market forces that were lined up against me!).

Now I was officially On Tilt, down about 90 pips on the day (even after winning 15 pips on my first trade) AND I WANTED MY MONEY BACK RIGHT NOW!!!!!

The next trade I put in an order for 2 mini-lots (my account was sitting at around $850 to start the day, and I'm down to around $760 at this point…waaaay too small an account to justify 2 minis).

Once the trade started to move against me (and believe me, it didn't take long) I moved my 20 pip stop down to 30 pips, then to 40 pips, all the time screaming at my computer, my platform, the Gods of Forex and anyone else I could think of to quit torturing me and give me a winner.

I finally bit the bullet and closed that one out at – 47 pips (times 2 mini lots) for another $94 lost and a $666 account balance.

That $666 figure should have been a sign to run away, but I ignored it.

Now I'm in a blind rage and not only am I not thinking clearly, I'm simply no longer thinking period.

I took another trade, and I can't even tell you why I decided to Buy or Sell. Once you're in full-on Tilt mode, rational thought is what other people are doing. I'm just reacting.

I sold the EUR/USD with 5 mini-lots, which pretty much ate up more than 80% of my available leverage. If I blow this trade, there isn't going to be much left to trade with in this account.

I was just wanting to score 20 pips. That would have equaled $100 and would have gotten me back about halfway to where I had been when I started the day.

But of course that didn't happen. I quickly went down 10 pips, and had I been capable of rational thought, I would have dumped he trade, eaten the 50 bucks, and spent the rest of the day banging my head into a wall or a door or something.

Instead, I watched as the trade moved slowly but surely away from my entry price. I was down 20, 25, 30, 40, 45, back to 40, then 35, quickly down to -60, and at that point I simply got up and walked out of the room (something I should have done about 3 trades back).

I didn't have a stop loss in place, but at this point I was so distraught I didn't care. I figured I'd blown up the account at this point, so I might as well let the trade run it's course.

And that's exactly what it did. A few hours later my broker closed out the trade for me and returned what was left of my margin (which was not very much).

I didn't cry, even though I wanted to. I gave myself a couple of days to calm down and then called on a long time friend who I knew had made a fortune trading in commodities. He's the guy who set me straight and got me back on my trading feet.

And here I am today, happy, healthy (mostly) and still making a nice living from my trading.

I still wrestle with those trading demons from time to time, and when I've banked a couple of unexplainable losses in a row, that little voice goes off in my head telling me to double up and get it all back on the next trade.

But I've learned to ignore that little voice, and approach trading as calmly and rationally as I possibly can, following the plan I've laid out for myself. It wasn't easy getting to this point, but I learned a couple of tricks I used on myself to help me limit the self-inflicted damage, and I'm hopeful that these little tricks will work for you as well.

Sensible Forex

Trick #1—Just Walk Away

I admit, it isn't much of a trick, but it's the most effective weapon you have in your arsenal to keep you from compounding on the mistakes you've already made.

In the beginning, I had a 3 Losers Rule. If I lost 3 trades in a row, I got up and walked away, ceasing my trading activity for the day. If you're a newer trader, and you don't have complete mastery over your trading system (meaning you don't know enough about it to have complete faith in its effectiveness) then you should give serious thought to adopting the 3 Losers in a Row Rule.

Today, I'm not so stringent with this requirement, simply because I know that I can get caught in a tight range on occasion and end up with 2 or 3 quick losers, but I also know that all I need is one winner (following my rules explicitly) to make it all back. But this goes back to having a tremendous amount of Confidence in both my own skills and in my chosen trading system.

But until you reach the same place where I'm at, just walk away after 3 Losers in a Row. You'll have limited the damage done to your account, and when you return tomorrow, it won't take a lot of effort on your part to erase the damage.

Trick #2—Switch Methods Temporarily and Scalp

Earlier I told you to find a method and stick with it, so you might think this next trick is more than a little hypocritical on my part.

Trust me, it's not.

You're in an extreme situation, trying to pull yourself out of the Loss Spiral. Extreme conditions sometimes call for extreme measures, including ones that are exactly the opposite of what you've been told (or taught).

In this case, you've banked a series of losses and you're account is depleted, perhaps even in danger of closing. Your confidence in yourself and particularly in your trading system is shot.

You can get it all back, simply by switching from your normal trading method and trading style and adopt a temporary new attitude.

You're now going to do a whole lot of 5 pip scalping.

5 pip scalping is exactly what it sounds like: you're going to get into trades off the short term charts, preferably the One Minute charts, and you're going to close out your trades every time you reach +5 pips.

Nothing succeeds like success, and nothing will build back both your confidence and your account balance than by using a High Percentage scalping Method and banging out a bunch of 5 pip winners. Very shortly you'll begin to realize that you had the trading skills all along. You just got yourself caught in a trading trap, and you paid a heavy price getting out of it.

But it wasn't the end of the world. You still can trade, and even though it may take you a few days (or weeks) to erase the damage you did to yourself, you can and will get back to break even soon enough, and then you can go back to your original trading method and pick up where you left off.

Or you might just decide to be a 5 pip scalper for the rest of your trading life.

Sensible Forex

Trick #3—Bite Sized Pieces

This trick works hand in hand with Trick #2. If you've suffered one of those monumental meltdowns and are looking at having to get back several hundred or even several thousand dollars just to reach break even, it can oftentimes look impossible. Sometimes you'll think your only solution is to wire more money into your account and pretend the loss never happened.

While that is certainly one solution, the better approach is to simply trade until you get that money back. Following this path has a two-fold benefit:

1. You are actually getting your losses back, instead of hiding them behind a new deposit, and
2. By trading yourself back into profit, you'll build your Confidence to the point you really will be bulletproof in the future. No matter what else may happen to you down the road, you'll be able to look back on the experience and remind yourself that you're a pretty good trader after all, and no matter what kind of trouble you may be facing in the markets right now, it's nothing you can't ultimately handle.

The problem with trading yourself back to even is that most of the time you are looking at a fairly sizeable amount you'll need to earn from your trading, and that figure can be intimidating to the point you begin to think your task is impossible.

So trick yourself by breaking that amount you lost down into "bite sized pieces." Let's say you lost $500 on a $1,000 account. With the new Leverage Rules in place here in the U.S., your options are already pretty limited (meaning you aren't going to be placing a 5 mini-lot trade and hoping for a 100 pip score to get back to break-even in one trade).

But instead of thinking of it as $500, think of it as $25 and 20 days. Meaning if you trade a single $1 mini-lot and shoot for 25 pips each day (or Five 5-Pip-Scalp Trades) the loss is now much more manageable.

You are no longer concerned about earning back $500. All you need to worry about is that first $25, and even there all you should be focusing on is that first 5 Pip Scalp.

A journey of a thousand miles starts with the first step. Quit worrying about your destination and focus on the trip itself. You'll get it all back eventually, and in the process build yourself into a lean mean trading machine.

Chapter Four

30 DAYS TO A MORE CONFIDENT TRADER

While a lot of what you're going to read in this chapter is redundant, I know from experience that a lot of you benefit greatly from having the previous material summarized and restructured into a Plan you can follow.

So here goes.

If you follow the plan I'm about to lay out, 30 days from now you are going to be 100% more confident in your skills as a trader, and that confidence will not only continue to grow, it will ultimately translate into a larger trading account.

Obviously, every person who reads this is coming into this plan with a different skill level, and a different background in terms of trading results. So if the numbers I throw out here are simply too small to hold your interest (meaning you tend to average more pips per session that what I'm suggesting) then go ahead and formulate your own numbers.

The same goes for those of you who simply aren't having ANY success in trading. Instead of trying to hit the daily numbers in my plan, adjust them downward to something that is both reasonable, given your experience, and yet just aggressive enough that you can have a sense of accomplishment should you hit your target at the end of the month.

First things first—when I talk about a 30 day plan, I'm talking about 30 calendar days, or one month. Within those 30 days, you should have 20-22 trading days. So when you are doing the math involved, use the actual number of trading days, not the number "30."

Step One in this plan is to choose a Pip Goal to shoot for. As mentioned above, you should choose a goal that is both reasonable and somewhat aggressive. Don't choose a number like 1,000 pips if the best week you ever had in your life was 75 pips. That's both unreasonable and overly aggressive.

For many traders, earning 100-150 pips a week is well within their abilities, so unless you simply never win your trades on anything that resembles a consistent basis, a figure within that range should suffice.

So let's say you can usually make 100 pips in the course of a week, and you have 22 trading days in the upcoming 30 day span. Since 100 pips a week equals 20 pips a day, 440 pips is a nice target to shoot for. But the idea is to be reasonable yet challenging to yourself.

Sensible Forex

So whatever number you land on, add an additional 10%. If your first target number was 440 pips, add another 44 pips to your total (10%) for a new target of 484 pips.

Step Two is to divide your Pip Goal by the number of trading days in the month ahead. In our example, 484 pips divided by 22 days equals 22 pips per day.

This makes your daily target 22 pips each day.

How you go about achieving your 22 pip daily goal will depend entirely on how you choose to trade. If you are a scalper who likes to jump in and out of trades with 5-6 pips per trade, you are going to need to net ahead at least 4 winning trades each day.

If you take a longer term approach to trading (meaning you prefer to hold on to your trades until you've made 20 or more pips), all you need is one winning trade a day to hit your goal.

But the idea here is to trade until you hit your target each day.

Of course, since there really are no guarantees involved in Forex trading, there may be days when you end up sitting on your hands and not taking a trade simply because the markets are absolutely flat during the time you are trading.

There are going to be days like that, and when you run into one of them, you merely recalculate your numbers, increasing your daily goal by a pip or two over the remaining trading days so that you stay on track to hit your target at the end of the 30 days.

Along those same lines, depending on how you trade, you might find yourself in the enviable position of making more than 22 pips on any one trading day (I've entered trades and before I even had the chance to set my stop and my profit targets, price took off like a rocket and I found myself up 30+ pips on a trade where I was hoping to make 10 pips and get out.

Learn to cherish those days.

But under no circumstances do you need to keep trading until you've lost a sufficient number of pips to get you back down to your daily goal. Bank every one of them and keep them in reserve in case you run into another one of those flat days.

Also, in the event you exceed your daily goal by some substantial number, resist the urge to reduce your future daily targets. Try to keep your daily number as consistent as possible, raising it if necessary, but never reducing it.

Step Three is to make full use of the Trade Justification Form for all your losing trades. Get your spouse or another trader to help you here by keeping your feet to the fire and forcing you to risk embarrassment by deviating from the rules of your trading system (or the generally accepted common sense rules that govern all forms of trading).

Step Four is to limit yourself to just 2-3 hours of trading each day. 2 hours is better simply because the longer you trade each day, the more fatigued you become and the more likely you are to start making mistakes. If you've been spending 4-5 hours a day (or more) in front of your platform, the odds are that forcing yourself into a more limited time frame for trading will benefit you in the long run. With less time to trade, you will have fewer trade opportunities (depending on the system or method you are using) and will not have the luxury of blowing off a signal through inattention or laziness.

Of course, scheduling those 2 hours during the London or NY sessions will give you the best shot at finding the best trades, but if those hours are simply unavailable to you, do the best you can with the time that you do have for trading.

Step Five is now simply to start trading. Put this plan into action.

And when you are trading, stick to the plan!!!

Don't get caught up in the emotions related to trading. If you end the day short of your goal, or worse yet, with a loss (gasp!) don't switch into Revenge Mode and try to get it all back on the next trade. Just go back to Step Two and revise your daily goal for the remaining trading days.

If you end the day up, recognize that you are dealing with the extra endorphins in your system that your brain releases when good things happen to you. In trading, this translates into exuberance, and can lead to what Alan Greenspan once termed "irrational exuberance." This can be as deadly to your account as Revenge Trading, as you begin to feel like you can't lose, and your desire to keep those endorphins flowing can lead you into over-trading in an attempt to keep the good times rolling.

You have a plan. Stick to the plan.

So let's fast-forward 30 days, to the end of your first month of Trading for Confidence.

If you made it through the month and made your overall pip goal, now is the time to reward yourself. That doesn't mean you run out and lease a Ferrari (unless your trading earned you a cool half million or so).

Pull a small amount out of your account (or better yet, out of your savings account or your paycheck or wherever) and treat yourself to something you enjoy. Go out to someplace nice for dinner. Pick up a new CD from your favorite group. Go to the movies.

Just keep in mind that whatever it is that's funding this treat came from your efforts as a TRADER! You made some extra cash due to your efforts, and you deserve this reward.

Traders who are consistent winners do this for themselves on a regular basis, and the sense of pride they (and you should) have when they treat themselves should work as a motivator to keep you following this same path.

And think about this for a moment—you just completed a full month of trading profitably on a consistent basis. All you did was follow your own system rules, stopped making dumb mistakes that are self-defeating and followed a real trading plan.

How does this make you feel?

That's a rhetorical question. I know how it makes you feel. Probably for the first time in your life as a Trader you can actually see how you can use Forex Trading to achieve all the financial goals you would otherwise not meet if you had to rely upon your paycheck.

And isn't that what we're all trading for in the first place?

So now that you have a successful month under your belt, where do you go from here?

Well, if following the 5 Step plan above worked out well for you, why not put together another plan for the next 30 days?

And when those 30 days are up, put together another plan for the next 30 days, and so on.

Sensible Forex

You can literally plan yourself right into the position where you are making more money from your trading than you are from your job. I'm not telling you to quit your job right now. But think back to the Bootcamp participant I mentioned in an earlier chapter. Keep doing what you're doing for a year or two until you've banked a couple of year's worth of your salary.

Then decide if staying on that job is making you money or costing you money.

Most of the people who are reading this book are Americans, and as an American, you are hard-wired for instant gratification. We all want what we want *now*, not next week or next year.

But by taking a reasonable yet somewhat aggressive approach to your monthly goal setting, you're going to see regular and impressive gains in your account. Just keep working towards your interim goals, and ultimately you'll wake up one day and find you've hit your overall goal, whatever that might be.

It just takes time. So let time work its magic, and you just keep plugging along.

Of course, there is the possibility that you did not hit your first 30 Day Goal.

That's okay.

You're new to this style of trading, and it might take you a while to really get into the swing of things.

The question, though, is did you end the 30 days ahead of where you started?

If you did, then you still have reason to celebrate. You ended the month up, and there is an enormous group of traders who cannot say that. In fact, there are very few traders who manage to have a month where they finished up in profit.

So you should be celebrating that. You've moved into one of the upper echelons of trading. You just need to spend some time reviewing your month, and your goals, and see if perhaps you we're too aggressive in your goal setting. Maybe you need to revise your goal down to an easier number to hit, and then try again for another 30 days.

And if you ended the month at a loss?

First, realize that most traders are in the same place you are right now. So don't feel like you are a failure. There are likely one or two reasons why this happened, and both can be fixed.

Reason Number One is that you kept making the same kinds of mistakes that are covered in the TJF. Review your month's worth of TJF's and see if you can isolate where you are having trouble. Once you've identified your weak spots, make a concerted effort in the next month to break those habits.

Reason Number Two is that the trading method you are using simply isn't a consistently winning trading method. Of course, if you're breaking the rules covered in the TJF, you probably aren't trading according to the rules of your own system, so you really didn't give it a chance to work for you.

But if you're doing everything right with your trading, you might need to investigate some other trading method that will give you a better chance at success. In the Appendix of this book, there is a link to a webpage where I break down a few different trading methods, and you might find that one of those methods is better suited to you than the method you are currently using.

But whatever you do, don't give up! Put together another 30 Day plan and give it one more try.

Chapter Five

USING ADVANCED SUPPORT AND RESISTANCE FOR ENTRIES AND EXITS

In "Survive and Prosper" I spent some time going over how and where to find various levels of Support and Resistance on your charts, based on "historical" levels that had proven to be solid S&R.

You could easily use only that information and do very well for yourself as a trader.

Sensible Forex

But in the time since I wrote "Survive and Prosper" I've run across a pair of MT4 Indicators which draw additional lines of Support and Resistance on the charts, and which have proven themselves to be very effective in identifying those prices on the chart where momentum will stall and price will oftentimes turn around.

And yes, I will give you both of these indicators for free on the Download page of my website...just check in the Appendix of this book for the link.

FiboPiv

The first indicator is called the FiboPiv. The FiboPiv will draw a Pivot Line on your chart, along with three lines of support (S1, S2 and S3) and three lines of Resistance (R1, R2 and R3).

You are viewing these pictures in black and white due to the price constraints involved in the printing of this book (using color pictures would raise the cost of the book by about $200 per unit) but you can see every one of them in living color on my website at www.sensible-forex.com/buyerspage.

But in spite of the lack of color, you should be able to read the designations for each line in this screen capture: the Pivot Level is about two thirds of the way down (at 1.3794). The three lines of Resistance are above that price point and two of the three Support lines visible below the Pivot line.

Pic. 5A

FiboPiv redraws these lines each day when your broker closes the daily candle (5 p.m. eastern time **for most** brokers). The calculation is simply based on taking the previous day's High and Low prices and then performing some basic multiplication and division functions.

But it's the accuracy of these lines that keep me placing a FiboPiv on the charts for every pair I trade. Quick war story: this morning was a terrible day for trading. No activity for an hour, then BOOM! A huge move of 80 pips (against the grain of just about every indicator out there) and then another hour of no activity. But on the EUR/AUD, there was a discernable upward trend in progress. It was just taking forever to cover any ground, AND price kept bumping into the R3

Sensible Forex

(Resistance 3) Level.

On the third attempt to break R3, the candle closed above the line, and I used that as my signal to Buy the E/A. 15 minutes later I closed out the trade at +12, as my other indicators began to give off Sell signals.

Had I not used the FiboPiv to identify this level of resistance, in all likelihood I would have missed the trade entirely and lost out on an easy 12 pips.

Pic 5B

In Picture 5B, you can see how FiboPiv works using a 1 Hour chart:

1. The candle above #1 is at 00:00 hours, which for this particular broker, means 5 p.m. eastern and the start of a new day. FiboPiv has reset, so the lines only apply to prices from #1 forward in time.

2. Notice the 08:00 candle touched the Pivot line, then fell back, closing below the Pivot. This is a common occurrence with the FiboPiv and many traders make a fine living playing "bounces" off these lines of Support and Resistance. While the 1 Hour chart shows only one bounce, shorter time frame charts will tell you exactly how many attempts it took for price to break through the pivot line.

3. Here price broke through the Pivot line, but spent the better part of 4 hours moving back and forth across R1. This demonstrates the "magnetic effect" I mentioned earlier, where price reaches a known line of Support or Resistance and seems incapable of moving beyond that line for an extended period of time.

4. At 14:00, price finally broke past R2, price moved up to just "touch" R3 and then began to fall back significantly. Again, this one hour chart shows only one 'touch' of the R3 line, and you should always look at lower time frames to get a true feel for how hard price had to work to try and breach this level of Resistance.

Sensible Forex

Pic 5C

This is a screen capture of the EUR/JPY 1 Hour chart. Notice the following:

1. The vertical line to the left of #1 marks the start of the new day (00:00). After initially moving up, price reversed and moved down and hovered around S1 for several hours.
2. At 07:00 price began to move up and bounced several times off the Pivot line, without ever having a candle close above that line.
3. At 10:00 price finally closed above the Pivot line, but failed to break R1 for 9 hours.

82

4. At 19:00 hours price finally broke through the R1 line and is now moving up towards R2.

Remember, FiboPiv is not really an indicator that gives you Buy or Sell signals (as such) but there are times when you want to see something take place vis-à-vis the FiboPiv before you take action.

This chart capture does not show it, but I had indicators on my screen giving me Buy signals around 09:00, but I ignored them due to the fact we were so close to the Pivot Line that I did not feel I had adequate room between my entry price and the Pivot line to justify the trade. I decided that I'd rather wait to see a candle close ABOVE the Pivot Line before I took the trade. As it turned out, on a shorter time frame chart (the 15 minute chart…Pic 5D on the opposite page) price closed above the Pivot line at 113.17 and I was able to close the trade out at +20 (my daily goal) several hours later (Pic 5E).

Given that the Pivot line held strong here for 3 hours (3 one hour candles) if you had been in a Buy trade and were well into profit by the time price reached the Pivot Line, you would have been justified closing out the trade at this time. And later, when price broke through the Pivot line, you would probably berate yourself for getting out "too early."

And this brings up an important point: If you make a decision, live with it.

Yes, there will be times you get out too early. But there have probably been plenty of times you stayed in too long and watched a good trade go bad before your very eyes. If you are using FiboPiv (or some similar type of indicator) and you are seeing price run into a virtual brick wall, you are perfectly justified in bailing out and protecting whatever profit you've already accumulated.

Sensible Forex

As my good friend Stu is known to say, no one ever went broke taking profit.

And if later, the trade finally takes off in your original direction, don't give it another thought. You made a decision, you took profit, and another trade is right around the corner. Focus on finding that next trade, not crying over what happened in the last one!

Pic 5D

Here's another example of FiboPiv telling you in advance where price was going to turn around.

Pic. 5F

1. On a 15 minute EUR/USD chart (Pic 5F), you can see that price made a few attempts before finally breaking through the Pivot Line and moving up;
2. It only took 3 candles to break R1 (35 pips away from the Pivot) and then the "magnetic effect" kicked in, keeping price hovering on either side of R1 for almost 3 hours;
3. After banging around below R1 for a while, price finally resumed it's march up to R2, where it again had difficulty breaking and remaining above R2;

4. An hour later, R2 was breached and price took the next hour marching up to R3, where it promptly stalled out and turned around...not a surprise since R3 is at the very top of the trading range many active traders are watching...watching and waiting to start selling once price reaches R3;
5. And based on the large number of sellers waiting in the weeds at R3, price then moved back down to R2, where it touched and bounced back into the middle of the range between R2 and R3.

As you are probably able to tell, most of the pictures in this chapter are screen captures of chart formations on or around March 2, 2011. I bring this up to make a point (again): I'm not jumping all over the place, looking for that one magical chart that makes whatever point I'm trying to make. These aren't "cherry-picked" examples. I could have gone back one week, or one month, or even one year and found plenty of examples, all of which took place over the course of a day or two.

What this means to you is that you can use the FiboPiv with confidence, knowing that on most trading days, price is going to behave exactly as FiboPiv predicts.

Pic 5G

Hopefully you aren't getting tired of seeing these FiboPiv examples.
I'm including more than just a couple because I want you to try and
prove to you what a valuable tool FiboPiv is to the professional trader.

1. In Pic 5G, a 5 minute GBP/USD chart, you can see that price
   broke through the Pivot line and then immediately fell into
   that "magnetic effect";
2. Price then shot up to R1, where the "magnetic effect" kicked
   in for a second time;
3. Price then spiked up to R2 (getting within 3 pips of actually
   touching R2), turned around and shot right back down to R1,

where again, magnetic effect kept price in a tight range just under R1;

4. Price then dropped right down to the Pivot line;
5. Where it bounced right back up to R1;
6. And price finally settles in around R1 for the 3rd time in 4 hours.

So does this mean FiboPiv ALWAYS works and ALWAYS gives out great signals for entries and exits?

Of course not.

There IS NO HOLY GRAIL.

NOTHING in Forex works perfectly ALL THE TIME.

EVERYONE LOSES A TRADE NOW AND THEN!

Those are **The 3 Truisms of Forex**. Keep them in mind the next time you get one of those breathless sales letters that promises instant overnight riches.

FiboPiv is no different. It works well most of the time, but will have days when it is really not much use to you. Today, for instance, when I got into the Buy trade on the EUR/AUD, it was after price broke up through the R3 price. There are no lines drawn by FiboPiv after R3, so once price enters the zone outside of the entire FiboPiv range, you're on your own looking for historic lines of support and resistance in order to find those spots on your chart where price is expected to run into "the wall" and the momentum behind your trade will stall, at least temporarily.

So how do I use FiboPiv for entries and exits?

Sensible Forex

It's simple enough.

For entries, my main concern is whether I am getting a signal at a time when price is too close to a FiboPiv line for me to make enough pips to justify the risk inherent in the trade.

What that means is that since I am a very "goal oriented" trader, I am looking for trades where I have a very good chance to make at least 5-20 pips. If I'm getting a signal to Buy the EUR/USD at 1.3250, and that price is 25 pips below the Pivot Line at 1.3275, I have no reason to not take the trade. There is plenty of room between my entry price and the Pivot Line for me to make part or all of my daily goal in this one trade.

However, if I get a Buy Signal on the EUR/USD at 1.3250, and the Pivot Line is at 1.3255, there is almost no room between my entry price and the Pivot Line to justify my taking on the risk of the trade. At least not until AFTER price breaks through and the candle closes ABOVE the Pivot Line.

By waiting until price breaches one of the S&R lines and for a candle to close on the "right side" of the line, I'm increasing the odds in my favor that my Trade Signal will now result in me making positive pips.

One thing to remember about these price breaks, though, is that often times these S&R lines seems to have a magnetic effect on price, and it can often take 5, 10 and even 15 minutes or longer before price breaks free from the S&R price and moves on into substantial profit.

So just because price broke through the Pivot Line and the candle closed on the right side for the trade does not mean you are 2 minutes away from massive profit. In fact, usually you have to sweat out a minor amount of whipsawing before the trade finally moves in your favor.

The reason for this is that there are hundreds of thousands of traders who are using programs similar to FiboPiv to draw S&R lines on their charts. And like those magical Big Numbers (the 00's and the 50's) which draw so many stop and limit orders, the S&R lines tend to draw a fair share of stops and limits themselves. So you just have to let price work it's magic and clear out the cluster of existing orders that surround each S&R line.

Using FiboPiv for exits (or as a signal to adjust your stop loss in the event you are trying to stay in a trade) is just a simple as using it for entries.

A couple of paragraphs back I mentioned the thousands upon thousands of traders who are using Pivot Points and S&R lines on their charts. They're seeing the same thing, more or less, that you are. They see price break up through the Pivot Line and their first reaction is to calculate how many pips it will take to get to R1.

For those traders who are trading for smaller pips (20 or less) they'll usually put in a limit order to get out just prior to R1 so that if price stalls just a couple of pips shy of hitting R1, they'll get out with a maximum amount of profit.

For those traders who are looking for the maximum amount of pips they can get in a single trade, they'll pay attention to how price reacts around R1. If price breaks up and through R1, they'll move their stop loss to break even and hope that should price turn around R1 will be strong enough to keep price from falling back to their entry. They then continue to monitor the trade and adjust their stop loss each time a new R level is breached.

One last thing to remember about the FiboPiv...FiboPiv will

automatically redraw the S&R lines as soon as the new daily candle opens. That means as of 5:01 p.m. eastern time, the lines you see stretching backwards into infinity (or at least to where your charts no longer provide any data) have absolutely NO RELEVANCE to the older data.

These lines only work on a forward basis until the close of the current daily candle (or backwards to the open of the current daily candle). Beyond that, they are meaningless. So if you see that two or three days ago price turned around when it hit the current R3, in all likelihood that is nothing more than coincidence. Unless you keep records or take screen captures of your daily charts, there is no way to say for certain that the FiboPiv drew a line at that price point on a previous date.

So don't bother doing any back-testing with this indicator. Your results will be useless.

Average True Range

A second and equally valuable tool for identifying those levels where price could/should/will stall and possibly turn around is the Average True Range (ATR) indicator.

The name of this indicator tells its entire story. It calculates the daily range from high to low of the pair you are watching, and averages those numbers over a period of days (usually 14). It then tells you what price you can expect to see as both a High and a Low, given the open and closing prices of the previous daily candle.

I'm not going to waste any time going into the math behind this indicator. If you're the type who really likes to see all the x's and o's drawn out on the chalkboard, do a Google search on ATR and you'll find plenty of sites that go into all the gory details behind the calculation of this number.

Instead, take a look at just a few of the chart captures I took today at the close of trading.

Pic 5H

In this screen capture and the next three that follow, there are 4 lines running horizontally for a short distance from right to left across the screen: (1) is the Top of the ATR Range; (2) is a point 80% from the top of that same range; (3) indicates the point that is 80% away from the expected bottom of the range; and (4) is the Bottom of the expect range for the day.

Here, using the GBP/USD 1 Hour chart, you can see how price moved down to the very bottom of the range, turned around and moved back up to the very top of the range, and then finally settled down between the 80% of Top and Top of the range.

You can also see that there were points around lines 2, 3 and 4 where price stalled out for a bit before continuing (or reversing, in the case of #4). These lines often act the same as the FiboPiv lines do…they act as a form of Support or Resistance, at least for a while.

Pic 5I

In Pic 5I, this is pretty much what we hope to see every day as traders. Price opens at 00:00 and immediately moves up to touch the Top of the Range. Price fails to break the range and then shoots right down to the Bottom of the Range. When price fails to break through the Bottom, it moves back up towards the middle and settles into a tight range.

There was no screwing around by price in this trade. Straight up, then straight down. If you could see this same formation every day for 3 months, you'd never want for anything financially the rest of your life (assuming you had the confidence to place the trades).

Pic 5J

Pic 5J reflects a chart setup you don't see every day, but you will see it on occasion.

By way of introduction, understand that the ATR bases it's projected Highs and Lows on the averages of prices over a set period of time, normally reaching back 14 days. This can lead to some odd looking ATR Lines, such as we see in 5J. As you can see, the LOW ATR line is actually ABOVE the opening price for the EUR/USD.

Price continued to move away from the range for several hours, but ultimately turned around and moved back inside the range. In fact, price ultimately moved up past the projected High by more than 20 pips before returning to the High price and ranging around it for the remainder of the day.

This chart merely underscores the point I've been making for years: nothing works perfectly all the time. Some methods and indicators work wonderfully until they quit working, and then they are all but worthless. But if an indicator or a trading method has some intrinsic value, it will begin working again (some day) so you should not abandon something that has been working for you just because it isn't working well today.

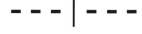

Pic 5K

One last ATR example, and Pic 5K is what you can expect to see on most trading days: Touching the High and then touching the Low (but not necessarily in that order) and then price will move into the middle somewhere and settle down.

These are just a handful of screen captures taken on the same date, looking at just a few of the available trading pairs. I didn't cherry-pick the best ones, and I didn't have to sit here for a week waiting for prices to fall within the ATR lines in order to make my point.
These are the kinds of results you get on many trading days when you rely on an indicator such as the ATR.

But remember, no indicator is perfect, and no indicator works perfectly 100% of the time. There are days when you can pretty much ignore the data you are getting from the ATR, either because prices are so flat there is no chance you'll see either the top or the bottom of the range, or prices are in such a strong trend, you blast past the high or the low and never look back.

But those types of days (flat and/or strong trending) fall into the minority. Most of the time you are going to see projected highs and lows hang tough, and price will normally turn around after getting into their neighborhood.

So you can use this information much like you can the S&R lines drawn by the FiboPiv. If price has reached the projected high or low of the day, you can expect to see price stall out and turn around, allowing you to enter a trade in the opposite direction of the trend that brought price to the high (or low) and make a handful of pips with very little effort and usually in a very short period of time.

In fact, I know of traders who place future orders, selling at the projected high and buying at the projected low prices, and placing 10-20 pip profit targets alongside very tight stops. This is the kind of trade you can place at 5:01 p.m. eastern each day, and it only takes a few minutes for you to set up a half dozen trades or more. At 5:00 p.m. the next day, you cancel the orders that did not execute and calculate your profits and/or losses on the orders that filled.

I'm not recommending you follow this strategy, but if you are one of those folks who is seriously pressed for time, this is the kind of trading strategy you can employ to take advantage of any small window of opportunity you might have, and with sound money management, you could turn this into a profitable way to make money as a Forex trader.

Chapter Six

"FOREX EARTHQUAKE"

By Raoul Wayne

A few years ago, a friend I'd met through a Forex forum decided to write an e-book detailing his knowledge of trading certain chart formations (those commonly known as Pennants and Flags).

Raoul wrote a tremendous book, and many people consider it the best short treatise on Chart Formation Trading they ever read, simply because he made the concept so understandable. He went so far as to have a website built and started to market the e-book, but soon lost interest in the internet marketing angle, and pulled down his website.

I did not know it at the time, but Raoul was suffering from cancer, and not too long after he shut down his website, he passed on. But before he died, he gave me the rights to his e-book and told me I was free to share this information as I saw fit.

So I'm sharing it with you here, word for word and using the original screen captures he used to illustrate his points. Learn from someone who really understood trading chart formation breakouts, because if you can master this skill, you can trade using nothing more than the information in this chapter and make a very nice living from Forex.

$$$$$$$$$$$$$$$$$$

The Forex Earthquake Trading Method

If you are looking for a trading "system" or method that consistently wins (in the neighborhood of 80% of the time) while at the same time allows you to limit your loss exposure on the few losing trades to a negligible few pips, then you've found exactly what you are looking for in the Forex Earthquake method.

A word of caution, though. This is not a trading method you can automate using trading software. It requires you to use a little independent thought and logic. But believe me, it's not complicated in the least, and once you've spent just a few minutes studying the charts I've included, you'll be as much of an expert in using this system as anyone else on the planet.

In the past few months, I have jettisoned all my other trading systems in favor of using his one method exclusively. Aside from the amazing consistency it provides, it also involves a particular "chart setup" that occurs as often as 2-3 times per day on virtually every single trading pair.

So if I'm looking to make a lot of trades in a day, this method provides that opportunity. If I'm only looking to make 1-2 trades a day, I can focus on a single pair and wait for the setup to develop, or trade a couple of pairs at one time, bank my profit, and call it a day.

And the best part of using this method is that it works no matter what the market conditions might be: volatile or ranging. The only difference in the two is that volatile times usually allow you to make more pips on a trade, while ranging markets are a bit stingier in giving up pips.

So let's get into the meat of the matter. Here's how you are going to become the most successful and profitable Forex trader you know.

To start, open your trading platform and open a 30 minute chart, using a pair of your choice. This system will work well on 1 hour and 4 hour charts as well, but I've found the 30 minute charts give me more trading opportunities while at the same time providing me with about 8 winning trades for every 10 I enter.

STEP ONE—SUPPORT AND RESISTANCE

It's not really a big secret that every successful trader incorporates the ideas of Support and Resistance (S & R) into their trading. But so many people new to trading think S & R is some mystical incantation that we mere mortals will never be able to grasp.

Not true. In fact, S & R is one of the easiest concepts to understand, and also one of the easiest "indicators" to spot on a set of charts.

Now let me prove that last statement to you.

Look at the chart below. See if you can locate the areas where the price of the currency ran into some difficulty in moving up (or down).

How many places on the chart did you find?

I found 10. I've marked them in the next chart.

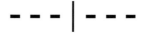

What you've just done is received your Master's Degree in Support and Resistance. If you can locate price levels on a chart where the item's price is having some difficulty moving up or down, you've located the price points where the market is demonstrating Support and/or Resistance.

And to clear up any confusion you might have over which is which, Support is the price level that provides a "floor" for the market price, supporting the price much like a floor supports your weight and keeps you from falling into the basement. So if a price is moving downward and hits a price level where the downward movement stalls out, it has reached a Level of Support.

The opposite of Support is Resistance, and Resistance works under the identical theory, but for prices moving in the opposite direction. If the price of an item is moving upwards, but reaches a price level where that upward movement stalls out, it has reached a point of

Resistance.

There are two more things you need to understand about S & R, and once you have these concepts mastered, you are ready to move on.

First, once a level of Support or Resistance is reached by the market, one of two things will happen. Either the price will break through that barrier and continue moving in that same direction or the price will reverse and begin moving in the opposite direction. This might occur within a few seconds (or minutes), or it might take several hours to happen.

But the price will not remain butted up against the S or R line forever. Eventually it will begin to move again.

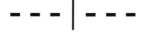

After 24 hours in which the USD/JPY ranged over 400 pips, things settled down a bit and the pair ranged within a 45 pip channel for about 12 hours before breaking out.

Secondly, a line you have identified as Support (meaning the downward movement of market price stalled at this price level) can change into a level of Resistance once the line of Support is broken and the price continues moving downward. The same is true of Resistance lines which are breached by market price. They then become lines of price Support.

So if your price breaks through a level of Support at noon and continues moving downwards for a while, when the price direction reverses at 3 p.m. and moves back up, it will normally find some difficulty in breaking past that old level of Support and moving up any further. In other words, that old level of Support is now a new level of Resistance.

*At 5 a.m. on March 15, the USD/CAD found resistance at around .9850
(1). After breaking through that resistance, the pair retraced and found
Support at .9850 (2). Around .9900, the pair found a bit of resistance (3)
which later turned into support (4).*

So far in my trading experience, I haven't found a 100% foolproof
way of figuring out in advance if the market is going to break through
an S or R line or reverse course. You just have to watch your charts
and react according to what the market does. But don't worry about
that right now. For now, all you need to do is open your charts to your
favorite pair and see how many levels of S & R you can spot. The
more you practice, the better you will get at locating these levels.

STEP TWO—ADD S & R LINES TO YOUR CHARTS

Now that you know everything there is to know about S & R, use
your chart tools to add lines on your chart to identify levels of S & R.

I've done this on one of my charts to give you an example to work with.

Arguably, there are a few other levels of S&R to be found on this chart, but I chose to only highlight those which were both obvious and which demonstrated numerous attempts by the pair to break through.

You'll notice I've made my S & R lines rather thick, and they are Yellow. This helps them stand out on the chart to my failing eyesight. You can make your lines any color or thickness you desire, as long as you can differentiate between normal graph lines on your chart and your S & R lines. So don't make them thin and black.

As time goes by and you become more comfortable with S & R, you'll probably find that you no longer plot these lines on your chart, as you can just glance at a chart and instantly plot the S & R lines in your mind.

STEP THREE—LOCATE AND PLOT POTENTIAL BREAKOUTS

"Breakouts?" you're probably thinking. "How am I supposed to even KNOW what a breakout is, much less locate one?"

Relax. It's so simple, even a cavem...(remainder deleted for copyright violation avoidance purposes).

Remember a short while ago when I told you that once a price reaches a level of support or resistance, it will eventually either break through the Resistance and keep moving up, or break through the Support and keep moving down?

This is what we're looking for. Areas on the chart where the price of the pair has consolidated into a very tight range and is trading right on a line of Support or Resistance. And while consolidating, the recent highs of the pair have dropped closer to the level of Support, and the recent lows of the pair have risen closer to the level of Resistance. Here's a picture of what we're looking for:

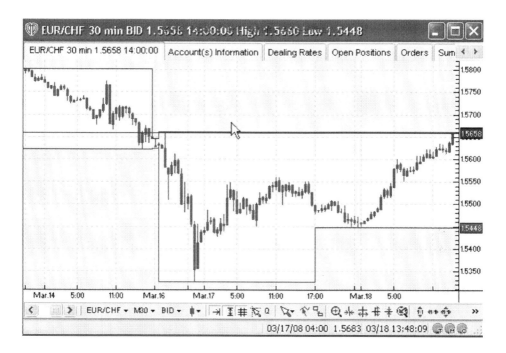

Notice how the price movement has created a sort of Pennant design on the charts?

This is a classic Pennant formation. You could also use the candles at 5 a.m. to form your 1st Pennant instead, and had a nice 50+ pip upwards breakout, then used the candles between 10 am and 4 p.m. to form a second pennant that would have captured the downward breakout that took place around 5 p.m. This is why I say there are several trading opportunities per pair each day.

We're looking for these Pennant setups to find our trades. I'll give you all the step-by-step details in a minute. First, I want you to understand why this particular chart formation is so powerful and why it results in us winning the vast majority of our trades.

Charts are nothing more than a visual representation of the activities of buyers and sellers in a particular market. When there are more buyers for a pair than there are sellers, the sellers have the advantage and can charge more for their product (currency) as the demand is greater than the supply. When there are more sellers than there are buyers, then the supply of the product (currency) is greater than the demand, and sellers are forced to reduce their price in order to entice buyers to buy.

What we are looking for are those times where over the course of several hours, the buyers and the sellers have forced the market into a position where the difference between what the sellers are willing to sell for and what the buyers are willing to pay is negligible, such as shown below.

Between 11 a.m. and 4 p.m. the price of the EUR/CHF ranged between 1.5550 and 1.5525, a 25 pip spread that followed 24 hours of trading with a 250 pip spread. That is an enormous compression which is going to build up pressure to break out of that tight channel in one direction or the other.

We're looking for these spots because they represent a sort of financial Earthquake Fault (and now the name of this book doesn't seem quite as lame as before, does it!). Sellers are pressing the price up and buyers are forcing the price back down, building up pressure similar to that which occurs underground when tectonic plates are trying to move against each other.

And what happens when the pressure created by these opposite forces is finally released?

You get significant movement. In the case of an earthquake, you might get a 3.0 shaker that rattles the dishes in your cabinet, or you might get an 8.0 devastator that levels tall buildings and creates tsunamis that kill thousands of people.

In the case of the Forex markets, you get a sudden and significant change in price. Sometimes it's only a few pips, and other times it can create a movement that lasts for hundreds of pips.

So that's what we're looking for: Those times when the buyers and sellers have given us all the ingredients necessary for one of these Financial Earthquakes to occur. All we need to do is watch for the first sign of a breakout to occur, then we ride her as far as she'll take us, banking pips the entire way.

So specifically, what you want to see is price movement where there are lower highs and higher lows being charted over the course of several hours. We are looking for three "lower highs" and three "higher lows" so that when we draw Pennant lines on our charts, we can more or less see a classic Pennant formation on our charts.

Using chart tools, draw two lines on your chart using at least three high points and three low points as guides. Your chart should look something like this:

My line drawing isn't 100% accurate (and probably never will be) but since we are just trying to find spots in the market where pressure is building between buyers and sellers, 100% micro-accuracy isn't vital to your success. Just getting it close is almost always good enough.

Once you have your lines in place, it's now a waiting game. What you're waiting for, exactly, is for your price to break through one of the two Pennant lines you've drawn on your charts. The rule of thumb I use is to wait for the candle to consistently maintain a 5-10 pip breakout before I place my trade. And the closer we get to the end of the 30 minute period (and the start of a new candle) the better.

If you are ultra conservative, you can wait until the first breakout candle closes and the next candle opens before placing your trade. You'll lose a few pips by waiting, but you'll also limit your loss potential even further.

Once price "breaks through" your Pennant, there is about an 80% chance it is going to keep moving in that direction. So if the price is moving up through your Pennant, then you would want to Buy that pair and follow along with the current trend. If the price breaks through the lower Pennant line, then there is about an 80% chance the price will continue in that direction and you would want to Sell and follow the downward trend.

Here are a few examples:

Sensible Forex

115

STEP FOUR—SET STOPS AND LIMITS

Once you're in a trade, the number one worry you have is "When do I get out, preferably with a profit?"

Remember those S & R lines I had you chart a little while ago?

That is your basic answer.

Assuming this is one of the 80% trades moving in your direction, you just wait for the price to reach the first point of support or resistance on your charts. You can pre-set a Limit Order with your broker so that when the price approaches that S or R level, an order closing out your trade is automatically executed and your profit is moved into your account.

Or, you can just watch your charts. If Support or Resistance holds and the price begins to reverse, you can manually submit an order closing out your trade and banking your profit.

But if Support or Resistance crumbles and your price continues to move in the same direction, you can just wait until price reaches the next level of S or R before you decide to stay in or get out of your trade.
But let's assume this is one of those trades that give you a head fake, starting out in one direction just long enough to get you into a trade, then reversing course. When do you decide enough is enough and close the loser out?

There are various ways you can set a stop-loss, and each has their pros and cons.

My personal favorite (if you can even use the word "favorite" when talking about tools to use in losing trades) is to plot a line where the candlestick closest to the tip of the pennant last touched one of my pennant lines. This is actually a point of support or resistance, as it helps form the Pennant line.

So if price breaks out one side of the Pennant and then reverses course after I'm in a trade, I'll get out if it breaks the other side of the pennant and past the level of the 3rd (or closest) candlestick that makes up the pennant line. In normal circumstances, we're usually talking about a swing of 20-30 pips tops. So the overall risk of loss is more than reasonable when we're looking at a trade where 80% of the time we're going to make 40 or more pips.

STEP FIVE—ADD A FILTER

This is actually an optional step, but it's one that helps me decide whether to set fixed Limit and Stop-Loss orders and walk away, or sit and watch for a while. I add a 200 Simple Moving Average to my charts to give me a longer term view of overall market direction. Most charts only display 50-60 candles at a time and trying to determine overall market direction is sometimes difficult. A 200 SMA removes that difficulty and gives me a visual idea of where the market is generally trending.

This is important, because if a Pennant breakout occurs in the direction that is OPPOSITE of the overall trend, more often than not, it is going to be a short breakout, and may not even reach the first level of support or resistance before reversing and rejoining the trend.

In fact, if the breakout occurs opposite the overall trend, and the first level of support or resistance is less than 20 pips away, I'll pass on the trade simply because there is a greater degree of risk of loss, and not enough of a reward to make that risk reasonable.

On the other hand, if the Pennant breakout occurs in the same direction as the overall trend, I have a fairly high degree of certainty that the trade is going to be a profitable one, and I will stick around and watch as the current price approaches the first level of S or R. These are the trades where 100, 200, even 300 or more pips can sometimes be up for grabs.

You don't have to add a 200 SMA to your charts to effectively use the Forex Earthquake method, but it will ultimately enhance your trading if you decide to add it to your charts.

Here, we see that the breakout was indeed in the direction of the 200 SMA, and was worth about 100 pips before reversing course and moving against the overall trend (a 300 pip move, I must admit. We couldn't forecast that one, but there are plenty of others that we will. Be happy with making 100 pips in about 8 hours and move on).

Here, the breakout occurred against the overall trend, and eventually would hit our stop loss. But the trade setup was a classic Pennant, with Lower Highs and Higher Lows, which normally leads to a solid breakout in one direction or another. But like I said before, we're going to lose an occasional trade. The secret is to bail out when our stop-loss is hit and not dwell on the loss. Another winner is lurking somewhere on your charts. Go find it and make some real money.

Summary

1. Open a 30 minute chart.
2. Plot Support and Resistance lines.
3. Find a Pennant formation in the chart with at least 3 points of contact on your trendlines.
4. Enter a trade when the current candle breaks through the Pennant trendline.
5. Set your stops where the nearest candle on the opposite side of the

breakout touches the opposite side trendline; set your Limit (profit) order at the next line of Support or Resistance. Or simply watch the trade develop and set a moving stop-loss to lock in part of your profits once the trade starts developing.

6. (Optional) Add a 200 Simple Moving Average line to your chart to give you a visual reminder of the overall market trend.

FINAL THOUGHTS

Utmost Precision and timing are required in occupations such as brain surgeon and bomb dismantler.

In Forex trading, not so much.

If you have a classic Pennant pattern developing, but find one of your points of contact is 3 or 4 pips away from making actual contact with your trendline, you can still use that as one of your 3 points of contact. All you are really looking for are spots on your charts where Lower Highs and Higher Lows are forcing the current price into a very tight range from which it will ultimately break out.

$$\$$$

I've given you the steps for finding the classic Pennant pattern. There is a slight variation on that pattern that works just as well, and you should look for this one while looking for Pennants.

This variation occurs when you make a series of Lower Highs, but your Lows remain more or less constant, or vice versa (Higher Lows but the Highs stay within a range of just a few pips). Chart #1 (EUR/GBP) on Page 14 above perfectly illustrates this point.

This chart formation can be even more powerful than the classic Pennant, simply because the "flat" side of this formation represents a very powerful level of Support or Resistance. Future prices can still go either way with this formation, so don't assume that the current strong level of S or R will hold once a breakout occurs.

But don't dismiss a potential trade simply because one side of your Pennant is flat, rather than angled.

$$$$$$$$$$$$$$$$$$$$$$$

In deciding to invest in this trading method, you probably read a statement I made along the lines that this system can give you upwards of 10 or more trading opportunities in a single day. Maybe you believed me on this point, and maybe you chose to ignore it or write the entire statement off as sales puffery.

When I finished writing this e-book, I turned on one of my trading platforms to search my charts for examples I could use to illustrate the various points made throughout. By design, I tried to avoid using the same chart for each illustration, choosing to use charts from as many pairs as I could to show the universal applicability of the Pennant trade.

I ended up using charts for 9 different pairs.

Look at the very bottom right corner of each chart, next to the three green balls. Those are the date and times each chart picture was captured.

Do you see where I am going with this?

Without having to go back any further in time than what was portrayed on my current charts, I found 9 trade setups (and frankly, on those charts, there are plenty of smaller Pennants which could have been marked and traded as well. I just plotted the large ones to make it easier for you to visualize what to look for.

Just ball-parking the figures, 8 of the trades were winners. Had you not set fixed stop loss and limit orders, but rather let the trades run their course, you could have banked around 1,200 pips in winning trades, and lost around 40 pips on the one trade (EUR/CAD) which didn't work out as planned.

All in about 36 hours, more or less.

This is not some pie in the sky, bass-ackwards analysis. This is applying a little economic common sense about supply and demand to a situation where the rules of supply and demand control every minute of every trading day.

And while every day won't bring 1200 pips in profit, 3-400 pip days are so common they become ordinary. And with those kinds of pips available for the taking, simply using conservative money management rules you can soon find yourself making more money from a day's trading than the majority of people on earth earn in an entire year.

And that's the whole point, isn't it?

So don't waste another day dreaming about the kind of lifestyle you could be enjoying as a professional Forex trader. Take some action. Open a real money account and start putting some of your new found knowledge to use. If you'll just follow the simple steps outlined in this book, you cannot help but make money, serious money, as a Forex Trader.

Chapter Seven

TRADING TRENDLINE BREAKS

I seriously considered titling this chapter "Trading Naked" since all you need is a brokerage account and a chart to make money trading this method. No indicators, no robots, no Magic 8-Ball.

All you need is your charts.

In several places in this book I've used the word "trending" to describe price action. Since it's such a common term, I never really bothered to define it. So to be safe, here's how I define trending as it relates to trading:

Sensible Forex

Price moves in one direction for a period of time.

Pretty simple, right?

It is simple. And so is the idea behind trading trendlines.

You find those spots where a new trendline has formed, and you enter a trade in the direction of the trend.

You stay in the trade until price breaks through the trendline, moving in the opposite direction of the current trend. [Note: This is what we call a "Trendline Break."]

Then you exit the first trade, and enter a new trade in the direction of the new trend.

Since a picture is supposed to be worth a thousand words, here are a few thousand words worth of explanation, boiled down into a few screen captures.

Pic 7A

Notice the complete lack of indictors in Pic 7A. Just a trendline I added, running along the tops of the candles starting at 11:00 and running through 5:00, when price moved up and closed above the trendline. This represents the "break" of the trendline and the establishing of a new trend. This is also when you should be entering a Buy order.

Yes, it really is just this simple, but there is at least one rule you should apply when using these trendlines.

For a trendline to be valid, you need price to touch the trendline in at least 3 spots. Since there will be plenty of times when you open your charts and see the beginnings of a new trend forming (but after it is too late to enter the trade safely) what you are looking for are two points where you can draw the trendline so that price touches the trend, and then you want that third ouch of the line to give you confirmation that the trend really is a trend.

Put another way, two touches of price to line does not a trendline make.

You want that 3rd touch before you have a valid trendline.

But don't make a mistake and think you need to see three touches before you can place a trade. The first candle to close on the opposite side of your trendline is your signal to Buy or Sell. After you buy or sell, you can then draw a trendline a soon as you see enough candles to allow you to draw a line with two "touches" and then you wait for touch number three for confirmation.

And as soon as price breaks through and closes on the other side of your new trendline, you exit your first trade and enter a new trade in the opposite direction (meaning if you were in a Buy trade, you close out that trade and now enter a Sell trade).

There are days where you can follow this pattern over and over and over again, closing out one trade in profit and entering a new trade when the current trendline is broken.

Pic 7B

1. In Pic 7B, you can see at #1 there were two touches of the trendline, along with the third touch for confirmation, all within the first 3 candles. This makes this an established trendline.
2. Since you are looking at a black and white picture, you might think that the candle located at #2 closed above the trendline. It didn't. This is one of those uncommon situations where price "gapped" upwards, meaning price jumped in the milliseconds between the close of the previous candle and the opening of the new candle. This candle closed below the trendline, as did the next three candles.

3. The first candle that closed on the opposite side of the trendline closed just over 1.3740. This is where you would enter a Buy trade, and you can see that over the next few hours, price moved up above 1.3830, making this a +90 pip trade.

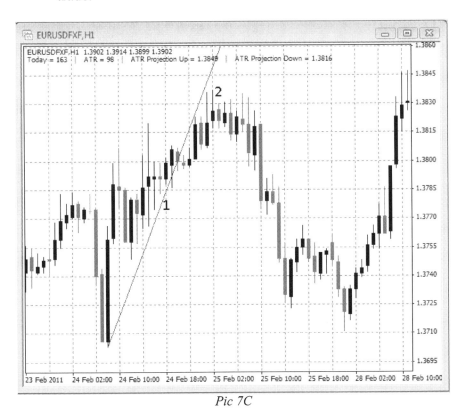

Pic 7C

Pic 7C raises an interesting dilemma: what if you enter a trade on the Trendline Break, only to have price move against you?

1. You can see the Trendline Break occurred above #1, at a price of about 1.3800. Because the previous trend was UP, this is your signal to SELL the E/U.
2. Over the next 10 hours, price moved up from 1.3800 to as high as 1.3840, leaving you 40 pips down on the trade. HOWEVER, notice that price NEVER ONCE closed on the opposite side of the trendline! In fact, it appears that price never even crossed the trendline. When this happens, you stay in the trade (if you have the guts to stay in a losing trade for an extended period of time!) As long as price stays on the "right" side of the trendline (meaning on the same side as your trade) you are still in a good trade. It just doesn't feel that way, since you're upside down on the trade at the moment. And in this case, your patience was rewarded with a 90 pip move into profit.

Pic 7D

In the previous screen captures, you've seen how trendline breaks work on the 1 Hour charts. They work just as well on most of the smaller time frames, and simply because you see more candles on those charts (1 hour chart = 1 candle, 15 min. chart = 4 candles, 5 minute chart = 12 candles) you will ultimately see more trendline breaks and find more trading opportunities.

1. In Pic 7D, you can see the first trendline shows price is moving UP.
2. A small candle closes below the trendline at around 1.3830. This is your first SELL signal.

3. 8 candles later, price finally closes above the current trendline at around 1.3770, for a 60 pip gain. You close out Trade #1 for 60 pips profit, and enter a BUY trade for Trade #2.

4. Things don't go so well here, and 8 candles later, price closes below your current trendline at around 1.3770, where you lose the trade at essentially break-even. You now enter a SELL trade for Trade #3. You can see I've drawn a SELL trendline just above #4, in anticipation that price would continue to move down and in the hope that I would get that 3rd "touch" making this a confirmed trendline. That never happened. Price broke my unconfirmed trendline within 2 candles and began moving away from my entry. Sometimes this happens, and when you have your preliminary trendline broken by price before you get the confirming 3rd touch, GET OUT OF THE TRADE! That third touch is supposed to CONFIRM you are in a proper trade, and when price falls apart before you get that 3rd touch, guess what? You aren't in a proper trade! So bail as soon as possible and wait to see what happens with price after your exit before you get back into another trade.

5. Here, price broke back through the trendline we'd drawn earlier for Trade #2, and we treat this as a BUY signal. We get an entry at about 1.3815, and price takes off like a shot after that, rising as high as 1.3915 before falling back a bit to the current price of 1.3902. As you are up over 80 pips on this trade, this would be a good time to set a stop-loss well into profit (somewhere around +50 or +60) and let the trade continue to run. Since this is a 15 minute chart, you are only going to get 4 candles an hour, so check back every 15 minutes to see if price breaks and closes below your current trendline, giving you your exit signal. But at a minimum, you should lock in a big chunk of that gain, to have something decent to show for your efforts today.

Pic 7E

In this example, we are looking at a 5 Minute E/U chart.

1. In #1 on Pic 7E, you are in an upward trend, as designated by
the trendline. Price breaks through the trendline at about
1.3828, giving you a SELL signal. But price then meanders
back up towards the trendline, but never crosses or closes on
the other side. So you are forced to ride out a 40-45 minute
period of inactivity, most of the time while down 2-5 pips on
the trade. However, the 9:15 candle closes down and signals
the start of the new downtrend. After 4 candles, you have the

3 touches of the line you need to confirm it is indeed a downtrend.

2. At approximately 11:10, price closes on the upside of the trendline, at about 1.3770, giving you your exit signal and a profit of about 57 pips (depending on your spread). You might notice that this trade is the same as Trade #1 in Pic 7D, above. Had you been trading on the 15 minute charts, your entry would have been 2-3 pips earlier than on this 5 minute chart, but that is not always the case. Oftentimes, the 5 minute chart gives you a better entry when a new trend begins quickly and moves with strength...by trading of the 5 minute chart, you would normally get a much earlier entry than you would by waiting for the latest 15 minute candle to close. So don't leave here thinking the 15 minute chart is always better than the 5 minute chart for trendline trading. Both have their positive and negative attributes.

Pic 7F

And just to show you that trend trading is not all Rainbows and Unicorns, I present Pic 7F…or as I like to call it, Mama said there'd be days like this!

1. You'll have to trust me on this one, but there were 3 touches on the downward trendline that occurred earlier in the chart, but too far away for me to include and still be able to show the upcoming train wrecks. You can see the candle at 11:10 closes above the first trendline, signaling an exit from a very

profitable sell trade, and a new entry (Trade #1) in a BUY trade.

2. At 11:50, price broke down through the trendline and closed 6-8 pips below our entry. Since we had a break of the trendline, we close out Trade #1 for a loss, and enter a new SELL trade (Trade #2) at about 1.3767.

3. At 12:15, our SELL trade was officially dead, as price broke up through the trendline, and we exited with about a 20 pip loss. We also entered a new BUY trade at 1.3785. And for a few minutes, we actually saw almost 10 pips in profit before the trade collapsed and headed back down below our trendline (again!), taking us out at about break-even (1.3785). Since we are in it to win it (or at the very least, we're masochistic gluttons for punishment), we enter a new SELL trade at the same price.

4. Finally, our hard-headedness is rewarded when price breaks over the new trendline, closing us out with about 20 pips in profit, and gets us into a new BUY trade that moves and stays in profit for at least 60 pips.

The point of this example is to show two things: First, you aren't going to win 'em all. And second, don't give up after a couple of trades, especially if your "losses" aren't much worse than break-even or a couple of pips to the downside. Plenty of people would have thrown in the towel after the third trade went nowhere, and sometimes that is the right move, particularly if you are prone to going on tilt after a couple of losses.

But in this case, all you really ever suffered was a 20 pip drawdown on one trade, so there should be no reason you couldn't stick with trading the trendline breaks.

Pic 7G

This picture isn't so much a "trendline break" as it is a cautionary tale: every now and then you're going to find yourself in a flat range trade. Pic 7G is a great example of a flat range trade. Price is flat, and it's ranging, but in such a tight range (15 pips, top to bottom, with most of the time spent in the middle of the range) that you really can't draw many trendlines.

Unfortunately, there is no way to tell in advance if you are in one of these tight ranges, until you are already well into the middle of it.

So here is a tip on protecting yourself from these account-killing situations:

If you've just lost two trades in a row (and your losses are small…in the 2-7 pip range) stop trading, and draw two lines on your chart: one across the top of the most recent high and one across the bottom of the most recent low.

This will give you something to shoot for on your next trade: a breakout from either the high or the low.

In the interest of full disclosure, this will not work perfectly 100% of the time. The two biggest roadblocks are going to be either a small breakout extends the size of the range by just a few pips, or you are going to get a false breakout in one direction, then a complete turnaround in price and a true breakout in the opposite direction.

However, *most of the time* when price breaks out of this range, it will be a true breakout and you will be able to resume drawing trendlines and trading future trendline breaks.

Pic 7G demonstrates what you want to see when you find yourself stuck in one of these tight ranges. Price bounces around within the tightly defined range as demonstrated by the two horizontal lines drawn on the chart. But once price breaks through the bottom trendline, a new trend is established and a new trade (a SELL) is called for. Here, you would sell when the first breakout candle closed, at around 1.3843, and over the next 15 minutes price dropped 40 pips. If you held out until price broke the trendline, you would exit around 1.3823, for a 20 pip profit and a new BUY trade would be placed.

Pic 7H

Pic 7H is an example of the False Breakout mentioned just above. Price traded in a tight range, broke out at the top of that range, immediately returned into the range, and then broke out through the bottom of the range.

1. You can see there was a candle that closed just under the top of the range, then the next candle (a Doji) closed exactly on the upper trendline. Neither of these instances are a true breakout, so no trade was called for. But the next candle closed 4 pips above the upper trendline, and was a signal to BUY.

2. Sadly, price immediately turned around and moved back into the range. I use this as an exit signal, and ignoring the two Doji candles that once again closed on the upper trendline price, I exited the trade at 1.3902 for an 8 pip loss.

3. 6 candles later, price broke out below the lower trendline, which was a SELL signal. Sold at 1.3894, and exited at 1.3886, when price broke through the trendline established by price action after the breakout from the range. This made for a net gain of 0 pips (-8 and +8), but that's okay. I'd much prefer to zero out my losses and start fresh for the next trade than drag a loss along behind me, in search of a trade that will get me back above break even.

Chapter Eight

A FEW MORE CHART FORMATION TRADES

This is another chapter in the "Naked Trading" series, because once again these are chart formations you can easily spot without the use of any indicators.

When you first get started, you might find it useful to draw a line or two on your charts to help you spot these "naked" trading opportunities, but I seriously doubt if anyone will need more than a day or so of practice to become a virtual expert in picking out these next trading opportunities.

Sensible Forex

M's and W's

The formations we'll be examining here are known by a couple of names: one group likes to call them "M's and W's" while the other group calls them Double Tops and Double Bottoms.

Hardly any explanation is needed to describe a Double Top (or M) or a Double Bottom (or W).

When you find a spot on a chart, preferably the daily high, where price stalled, fell back, made another attempt to breach the daily high, and fall back a second time, you have a Double Top (M).

When you find a spot in the charts, preferably the daily low, where price stalled, moved back up, made another attempt to breach the low, and moved back up a second time, you have a Double Bottom (W).

I probably don't need to go any further explanation, but for those of you who still don't get the picture, in a Double Top, price moves up, like so: /

Then price falls back, like so: / \

Then price moves back up again, touching or getting extremely close to the high price set just previously, like so: /\/

And finally, price falls back again, like so: /\/\

That chart formation looks exactly like the letter "M" and the upper two points of the "M" which mark the spot on the charts where the High price was touched twice within a brief period of time (the meaning of "brief" being dependant upon the time frame of the chart you are using) are what make up the Double Top.

142

If you were to flip that explanation upside down, using two low points on the chart, you would then have a Double Bottom, or W, like so: VV

The two spots on the chart where price reached its low point in this sequence are what make up the Double Bottom.

The theory behind the Double Top is the same as behind the Double Bottom. Price made two attempts to set a new high or low price, and failed. Once that failure is established, a trade opportunity arises trading in the opposite direction of the top or bottom.

For instance, if a Double Top is Forming, meaning price has peaked, fallen back, and is now approaching that peak a second time, once price begins to retreat, you enter a Sell trade.

And the same holds true for the Double Bottom. If price reaches the bottom and pulls back, once it begins to approach that low price a second time, you need to be ready to enter a Buy order as soon as price begins to move back up.

Do Double Tops and Double Bottoms always work out so that once the High (or Low) price is touched a second time, a reversal in price is guaranteed?

Of course not.

But it works often enough that you can trade Double Tops and Double Bottoms with a high degree of confidence. What's more, when trading a Double Top or Double Bottom, the closer you enter the trade to the actual High or Low price, the smaller the stop loss you can use, and the less risk you have to endure during the course of the trade. I prefer to set my stop loss just a few pips (5-7) above the High or below the Low, so that any losses I take make a negligible impact on my account.

As for when you get out of the trade, every trade will be different, so there is no real hard-and-fast rule I can give you. But here are a few options, one of which will probably apply to the trade conditions you are dealing with at the moment:

1. Once your trade reaches +10, move your stop loss to break even. This makes it a "free" trade for you, and even if you get stopped out, you've lost nothing except a little time…just make sure when you place your stop you account for any commissions you might be paying to your broker;
2. Look for the most recent level of Support or Resistance that is in front of your trade. This can be a level that appears on your chart courtesy of an indicator like FiboPiv or the ATR, or it can be one of those "invisible" levels where price recently stalled out for no apparent reason;
3. Aim for the Big Round Numbers, such as the closest 50 or 00. Price normally will stall out once it reaches either of these levels, and is often a good spot to close out a trade before a bounce off the level occurs and you watch 10-20 pips of profit disappear, at least temporarily;
4. Fall back to the skills you learned in Chapter 7 and draw a trendline, exiting your trade once that trendline is breached in the opposite direction of your trade.

Next up are several charts that demonstrate the M's and W's (sorry, but I'm getting tired of typing "Double Tops" and "Double Bottoms") but before we delve into the charts, let me make two last points clear.

First, you can spot an M or a W anywhere on the chart, and the rules as described above will apply. However, the strongest of these trades occur when price is approaching either the daily high or the daily low. When you reach a daily high, either for the first time or at some point later in the day, it becomes the Daily Highs because Sellers take over at that point and force price back down.

The same holds true for the Daily Low. It's called the Daily Low because at some point, the Buyers took over and forced the price back up.

The point is, whether you are looking at the Daily High or the Daily Low, there is a group of traders out there (Buyer or Sellers, depending) who have a strong interest in protecting a position, and they express that interest by increasing their Buying or Selling activity and forcing price to move away from their positions (stop losses in about 99% of the cases).

When price makes the second attempt to break that High or Low, the Buyers or Sellers are still there, protecting their interests. So the same result is expected...price will move away from the previous High or Low.

And don't think for a moment that large institutional traders are not aware of this trading phenomenon and are not actively trying to set these trades up whenever possible. Traders will intentionally try to force price back up or down to create this M or W formation, just so they can exit their first trade and then enter a second trade, taking advantage of the upcoming price rejection.

You might as well join them and pick up a few pips in the process.

The other point I want to clarify before we get to the charts is the question I know most of you have, which is "how many pips can I expect to make on a trade like this?"

To that question, I have the one-size-fits-all answer of "it depends."

Sensible Forex

Your pip-profit expectation is going to depend on several factors, not the least of which is going to be the time frame you are trading.

An M or W formation on the 1 minute charts in most cases will return fewer pips than the same formation on the 4 hour charts. The reason for this is that fewer traders are watching the 1 minute charts and scalping handfuls of pips when they can find them. The bigger traders (banks, hedge funds, etc.) have armies of traders pushing around millions and billions of dollars based upon information derived from 1 and 4 hour charts (and daily, weekly, monthly, etc.).

So trading the second down leg of an M or up leg of a W on a 4 hour chart will in most cases return you far more pips then the same formation traded on a 1 minute chart.

But the same rules apply for exiting the trade...strong levels of Support or Resistance, stalling out near the Big Round Numbers, trendline breaks, all of these will apply on the 4 Hour chart just as they do on the smaller time frames.

So now that I have that off my chest, let's look at some charts.

Pic 8A

This is a fairly clear example of an "M" or Double Top.

1. You can see on the left side of the chart that price has been moving up, and eventually stalled out at 1.4035;
2. Price then retreated to 1.4023 or thereabouts;
3. Price then returned to test the high at 1.4035, only to be rejected a second time; and
4. Price then fell 45 pips, down to 1.3990. If you were trading in anticipation of a Double Top forming (the possibility of which became apparent as price moved closer to 1.4035) you could put in a future order Selling the EUR/USD at 1.4033 or 1.4034

147

(to account for whatever spread you might be paying your broker) and entered the Sell trade at the best price possible..

Pic 8B

This is the best "W" I've seen in a while. But there is one flaw here which deserves some discussion:

1. Price moves down and establishes a low at 1.3955
2. Price then retreats back above 1.3975;
3. Price then moves back down toward 1.3955 but does not actually reach that price; momentum stalls out 2 pips away at 1.3957…this is a common occurrence when you are dealing

148

with M's and W's. This type of trading is a lot more Art than it is Science, and you have to build in a margin of error when looking for these chart formations. Since the first 3 legs of the W are so clear, the fact that price fails to actually touch 1.3955 should not keep you out of the trade.

4. And if you took the trade at the close of that first candle on the second rejection (the 4th leg) you got an entry in the neighborhood of 1.3965 and enjoyed a nearly flawless run up in price to 1.4030, for a potential gain of 65 pips.

Not a bad score considering you don't have a single indicator on your charts.

Head and Shoulders

The final "naked trading" chart formation is called Head and Shoulders (and should not be confused with the popular hair care product of the same name.)

Simply put, a Head and Shoulders formation occurs when price establishes a high or a low, falls away, then establishes a new high or low, falls away again, then returns to the first high or low before falling away for a third time. That third price retreat is where you place your trade.

Like the M's and the W's, you'll see the occasional "perfect" chart setup where price stalls out in the exact same place for the first and third move. However, most of the time, price will only get into the near vicinity of that particular price level, and it is up to the trader to decide if "close" is close enough.

As I mentioned earlier, this kind of trading is more Art than Science, and your expertise in spotting these Head and Shoulder formations will improve with practice.

Also, Head and Shoulder formations will form both as Buying and Selling opportunities, so don't get too focused on only looking at only the top or only the bottom of your charts. You'll be cheating yourself out of some easy pips otherwise.

Pic 8C

We might as well start with a tough one (although there are even tougher chart formations that qualify as a Head and Shoulders formation, as you will see).

1. Price established a high at 1.4005.
2. Price then meandered back down into the 1.3960-75 range.
3. Price then shot back up and established a new high around 1.4035.
4. Immediately after touching 1.4035, price began its freefall, landing back in the 1.3960-75 range again.
5. Price finally broke out of the 1.3960-75 range, stalling out at 1.3990. By failing to reach 1.4005 like it did a couple of hours prior, price action prevented this setup from being a "perfect" Head and Shoulders formation. But the fact is, most Head and Shoulders formations are not "perfect" and in this case, the increase in price by 15 pip above the established range of 1.3960-75 caused the charts to give a solid "2nd Shoulder" on which to base a Sell trade decision. Once price began to retreat from 1.3990, a Sell trade is called for,
6. The entry for the Sell trade will vary based on Trader preferences. If you have a lot of faith in these chart formations, once price began its retreat from 1.3990, you are entering the trade. If you are a cautious trader, you recognize that once price re-enters that previously established range of 1.3960-75, it may not fall much farther. So either you enter a Sell trade above 1.3975 with an eye towards exiting at 1.3960, or you wait until price breaks below the low end of that previously established range (below 1.3960) and enter your Sell trade at that time.

Here, had you waited to enter until after the low end of that range was breached, you were rewarded with an 80+ pip move. That does not mean you are going to get 80 pips every time you catch a Head and Shoulders trade. In fact, far from it. You could end up with a much larger trade on your hands (hundreds of pips in profits) or you could end up with just a handful.

That's both the beauty and the infuriating nature of trading Forex. There are never any guarantees, so "you pays your money and you takes your chances," as the man once said.

Pic 8D

Here is another not-so-perfect example of a Head and Shoulders trade on a 1 hour chart.

1. Price moved up dramatically for several hours, and then entered a period of consolidation, with a High around 1.3385.
2. Price then dropped back to a low of around 1.3325, but almost immediately began to move back up.
3. Price peaked at a new high of 1.3450, but was unable to hold that position and was immediately forced back down 1.3415.
4. Between 3 and 4 is where things get interesting. After 12:00, price drops back down and touches 1.3325 (the low established at #2, above) then shoots back up and touches 1.3385, which is the same High that forms the first Shoulder. Aggressive traders would have a Sell order in place here, and price cooperates by dropping back down towards 1.3340, for a 45 pip gain. But the interesting part is that price again moves back up and briefly breaks 1.3385 before falling back down towards 1.3325. This second test of the Shoulder level (1.3385) is grounds for a second Sell order, and again price cooperates and drops down to 1.3325.
5. Making things even more interesting is price goes back up to Shoulder level (1.3385) a THIRD time, and still fails to clear that price level. This allows traders to place one more Sell trade when upward momentum fails and price heads back down towards 1.3325.
6. This time the 1.3325 level fails to hold, and price drops an additional 60 pips before finding some Support at 1.3265, a full 120 pips below the entry price at 1.3385. Once the lower Shoulder price level (1.3325) is broken, it's unlikely that price will return to 1.3385 again, and this Head and Shoulders trade is complete.

This is a very good example of the type of variations you can expect to see when trading Head and Shoulders formations. Yes, you might see a "perfect" setup now and again, but for the most part you will be dealing with a lot of "close" setups and you'll find yourself forced to make a few judgment calls here and there. But since these formations are so powerful, getting 'close" is usually good enough, so don't agonize over not hitting a previously established level down to the pip.

Pic 8E

Here is a Reverse Head and Shoulders, so called because the main price action is moving Down, not Up, so the Head and Shoulders are reversed.

1. Price fell from the upper 1.31 area down to 1.3085 (notice that there are several candles with wicks that reach past 1.3085, but each candle closes above that price. You can use either 1.3085 as your Shoulder level, or you can use the exact

lowest price…1.3076 in this case…all that really matters is that you can identify a price level where momentum stalled and price retreated from the current trend)

2. Price bounced back up hard over the next few hours, reaching 1.3150.

3. Over the next 7 hours price was in a freefall, twice touching 1.3055 before bouncing back up. This forms our Head, and you can see that price again reversed and moved back up significantly, falling just a couple of pips short of once again touching 1.3150.

4. Again, we have a situation where a candle (22:00 by my count) shot back down and touched the Shoulder level at 1.3085 before beating a hasty retreat back towards it's opening price. Traders who recognized a Head and Shoulders trade setting up would already have a Buy order in place at 1.3085 (or in the vicinity). Since price never actually touched 1.3085, an order placed at that exact price probably did not trigger, but once placed 3-5 pips away (1.3088-90) would be in the trade and stand to make as much as 60 pips, depending on when and where they exited the trade.

5. For those traders who were outsmarted by the market and missed their entry at 1.3085, they got a second bite at the apple a few candles later when price blasted down to the 1.3085 level (actually dropping as low as 1.3074).

6. Price turned right back around and moved back up past the 1.3150 level (where our previous shoulder stalled out) and ultimately earned more than 100 pips for their backers.

The sharp-eyed among you probably noticed something significant about this last chart hat had nothing to do with price action (actually, it probably had EVERYTHING to do with price action, but I'm not talking about the candles here).

Look at the date on the chart.

This Head and Shoulders formation began to form on December 22, and finally reached a point where traders could have made money on both December 24th (Christmas Eve) and again on December 26th (Boxing Day). Yes, the markets are open on both the 24th and 26th (as long as they don't fall on a weekend) but you really and truly need to have your head examined if you are putting real money at risk trading in the days surrounding Christmas.

Most traders take the last two weeks of the year off, and you should to. Why jump into trades when volume is low and the chance of getting slaughtered by crazy price action is high?

This chart was used simply to show a Head and Shoulders formation, not to suggest you should be trading over the Christmas holiday.

Pic 8F

Ah, if only every trade were as easy to spot as this one.

1. Price moves down and stalls around 1.3535 (the wicks show us price touched that level, even though the candles themselves closed around 1.3542)
2. Price retreats to 1.3570.
3. Price then moves down and sets a new low just a couple of pips shy of 1.3505.
4. Price then retreats to the exact same price as before…1.3570.
5. Price falls from that high, and gets within a couple of pips of where the first set of Shoulder candles closed, but is still 8-9 pips away from the lower level where price touched previously.

6. It is another judgment call on the part of the trader, but once price breaks up past 1.3570 and continues moving up, there is no longer any doubt. Traders would be Buying at 1.3571 and would have been rewarded with a HUGE gain, if they had the nerve to stay in the trade for 2-3 days. This marked the beginning of a 240 move up (the chart above only shows a tiny part) and not once was this trade ever in drawdown. Once it took off, it kept moving up for several hours before finally leveling off.

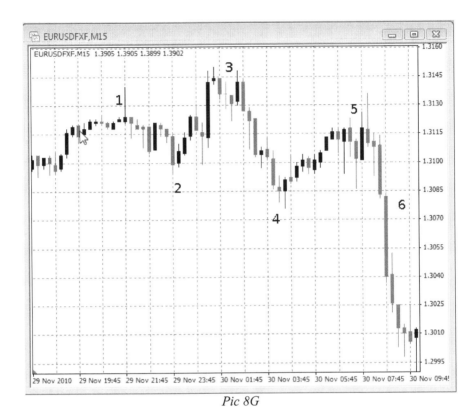

Pic 8G

Up until now, the Head and Shoulders examples have been pretty clear cut.

This example, not so much.

1. You can see that price moved up to the 1.3120 level (approximately) with one candle spiking as high as 1.3040.
2. Price then drops down to 1.3100 (with a wick one one candle down to around 1.3092)
3. Price then marches up to a new high just over 1.3145, and ranges around that level for 7candles.

4. Price then plummets down PAST our first shoulder low of 1.3100, reaching just past 1.3085 before leveling off.
5. Price moves back up to form a second (slightly lopsided) Shoulder at around 1.3118 (although price was considerate enough to spike up to 1.3136, getting within 4 pips of the spike/wick on the first shoulder). This price move would have been enough to get anyone except the most conservative of traders into a Sell trade.
6. But even if you missed your chance with that wicked candle, price eventually moved below our second Shoulder low at 1.3085, justifying a Sell trade which was quickly rewarded with 90+ pips profit.

This is a very good example of a lopsided Head and Shoulders. When you are trading, you obviously do not have the benefit of seeing the completed Head and Shoulders until well after the trade is over. So in the heat of battle, so to speak, you are forced to make these judgment calls on whether a second Shoulder has formed, since oftentimes price will not cooperate and move far enough in one direction to trigger any trades you might have lurking about in anticipation of just such a move.

This leaves you with two options: Either take the trades that seem to get close to your target price, or pass on the trade. There is no shame in passing on a trade. In fact, trades are like city busses; if you miss this one, don't panic. Another one will be along shortly.

Just don't beat yourself up if you miss taking a trade (or intentionally pass) and later find out you would have made some pips had you taken the trade. You'll get another chance shortly to take another trade. Just don't start fudging on the rules of your trading method or system to try and "force" the trade to fit your requirements.

Relax. Take a deep breath. You'll be fine.

Pic 8H

Consider this chart a palate cleanser, after that last example. A textbook example of what you'll see most of the time.

1. Price moves up and establishes a high.
2. Price moves back down a bit.
3. Price moves back up and establishes a new high.
4. Price moves back down, not quite to the same level as in #2, but pretty close.

5. Price moves back up and forms a second shoulder, which is slightly lopsided because price actually exceeds the high of Shoulder #1 by a few pips.
6. Price drops 200 pips after failing to get much higher than Shoulder #1. There are a couple of valid entry points, one being when price fell back and closed at 1.3925 (the 14:30 candle, if you're counting), the other being when price broker below the Lows established by the Shoulders (in the area of 1.3905).

This is the type of chart formation you'll see the most often, so study it closely and look for it whenever you're trading.

Pic 8I

If you're thinking I saved the best (or worst) for last, you're thinking correctly.

This chart is an absolute disaster, but ultimately forms a Head and Shoulders and gave astute traders the chance to make some easy pips.

So let's sort out what took place.

1. Price moved up (substantially) peaking at just over 1.4025. (a) There was a very fast spike up and then right back down, but no "new" high that would qualify as a Head was reached. (b)

This is almost a carbon copy of the move in (a), but again, no new high was reached. At this point, it is unlikely anyone is looking at this chart and expecting to see a Head and Shoulders formation.

2. The Shoulder low is established at 1.4015, and price action uses this level as Support 5 different times before price finally moves up and away from this support level.
3. A new high is reached at 1.4035, and now you can start to see a Head and Shoulders formation becoming a possibility.
4. This is where things get tricky. Price drops, and then (a) bounces right back up to 1.4035. If you've paid attention in the previous chapters, this is what kind of a formation? A Double Top (and the sharp-eyed amongst you probably noticed that this chart is the same one that appears earlier as Pic 8D, demonstrating the Double Top). This would justify a Sell trade as soon as it becomes clear that price is not going to break the level at 1.4035; (b) and price further cooperates with the Double Top analysis by falling right back down to the low set by Shoulder #1 at 1.4015, where it meanders around a bit before finally moving back up.
5. Price again reaches the general vicinity of the high set by Shoulder #1 (it missed an exact touch by 3 pips) and now you can see that you have a legitimate Head and Shoulders formation which also happens to enclose a Double Top.
6. And if you were looking for a Head and Shoulders trade on March 7 around noon (chart time) you were rewarded with a 30+ pip gain that was actually easy to spot, if you knew in advance what to look for.

And from here on out, you now know what to look for. A High or a Low, followed by a retrace and then a setting of a new High or Low, followed by a retrace and a return to the first High or Low. Once that previous High or Low is touched by price (or price gets close) it's time to send in a trade.

Like any other trading method, Head and Shoulders formations don't result in profits every single time. But they win frequently, and in pip amounts large enough to erase any bad taste left by a trade that fails to move into profit.

You won't see this kind of formation every day, and certainly not several times a day if you are trading the longer time frame charts. But it only takes a few seconds to spot one of these chart setups, so from now on when you open your charts, take a couple of minutes and spin through 3-4 time frames and see if one of these gems is setting up. Your account balance will thank you for it.

Chapter Nine

WORLD'S SIMPLEST 5 PIP SCALPING METHOD

For a book that was intended to help you build your confidence, it's spent a long time instead discussing various trading methods and systems.

But there is a very good reason for that (aside from the need to fill up some pages with content):

All of the methods discussed so far have an extraordinarily high win rate when compared to your average $97 Clickbank system.

And when your confidence level is suffering after slogging through a series of losing trades, there is no better prescription for a return to the Higher Level of Confidence you once enjoyed than winning a few trades in a row and washing off all that Loser Dust you picked up earlier.

And of all the methods discussed so far, none is any better than this ultra-simple 5 Pip Scalping System.

The Rules are easy to follow:

1. Trade the EUR/USD on the 1 Minute charts;
2. Apply the OsMA Indicator to your charts, using the "12,26,9" settings;
3. For Buy trades, enter as soon as the first OsMA bar closes ABOVE the "0" line;
4. For Sell trades, enter as soon as the first OsMA bar closes BELOW the "0" line'
5. Exit when you see 5 pips profit.

While this method will work with pretty much any pair, I strongly recommend you limit it to the EUR/USD, for two reasons: first, the spread on the EUR/USD is normally the smallest, no matter who you trade with, and this gets you to +5 on the trade much faster than with pairs that traditionally have a spread of 2-3 pips; and second, the EUR/USD is traditionally a pair that does not experience quick, wild swings in price, increasing the chance that any one trade will move 5+ pips after the OsMA "0" line is crossed.

Of course, all the usual rules of trading still apply: trade during times of higher volume (the London and New York sessions) and do not get into a trade right before a scheduled news release (it just isn't worth the risk). I've found the first hour of the London session (3 a.m. eastern time) and a two hour period after the U.S. session begins (9-11 a.m. eastern) are the most consistent, and have had plenty of days where I scored 5 out of 5 winning trades.

That does NOT mean you will win every trade during those particular hours. It just means I've found that this method works best during those 3 hour segments. Losses can and do still occur. But there have normally been more wins than losses, and I normally end the session with a positive pip count.

Other than that, there are no other limitations on the trade. Just get out at +5 and wait for the next trade to set up. Other than those random days when the EUR/USD is trending strongly in one direction, there are usually enough trades in any two hour segment to easily make your +20 for the day.

As for a stop loss, either apply a 10 pip stop-loss, or manually get out at either -10 pips, or when the first OsMA bar closes on the opposite side of the "0" line (this will usually save you 2-3 pips over waiting to see -10).

For myself, I usually set a daily limit of 20 pips, simply because I've reached that point in my trading life where I'm trying to develop some non-forex related interests, and by limiting myself to 20 pips (or 2 hours) of trading, I can achieve all of my financial goals and have plenty of time left over to pursue those other interests.

But more importantly for anyone who has just suffered a string of losing days, 20 pips a day is an achievable goal that allows you to start building up momentum, as well as your trading account, while also allowing you to manage all of those negative emotions that surface when you find yourself mired in a losing streak.

I know of a semi-professional poker player who follows the same path whenever he suffers through a few losing sessions. He normally plays $20/40 Hold 'Em, where the pots regularly exceed a thousand dollars.

But after he gets smacked around by the other players, he goes online and plays in a bunch of $2/4 and $5/10 games, against players of a lesser caliber.

All it takes is three or four winning sessions at his lower level, and he is back on his game and ready to resume playing in the bigger money games.

As he explains it, it's not about the money (and there is obviously a lot less at stake in a $2/4 game than there is in a $20/40 game).

It's about winning pots and reminding himself he really does know how to play the game at a very high level.

The same applies to Forex—the best way to break a losing streak is to rack up a series of smaller wins and remind yourself you really do know how to trade; you just got caught up in circumstances and needed to break free of that losing cycle.

Winning 4-5 trades in a single session, scalping 5 pips at a time, will go a long way towards breaking that cycle.

Here are three chart captures from last Friday. The first is from the opening of the London session at 3 a.m. eastern time. The next two are from 9 a.m. and 10 a.m. eastern time. Friday was a very good trading day, and this simple method worked like gangbusters. On days when trading is less active, this method still will work well, but you may see fewer trades, and you will definitely see smaller price moves than the ones demonstrated here.

But the purpose of these charts is not to convince you to trade this method. They are merely demonstrations of when and where you enter a trade (with the exit pre-determined at +5 pips).

Pic 9A

5 trades, 5 winners.

25 pips net.

What more need be said?

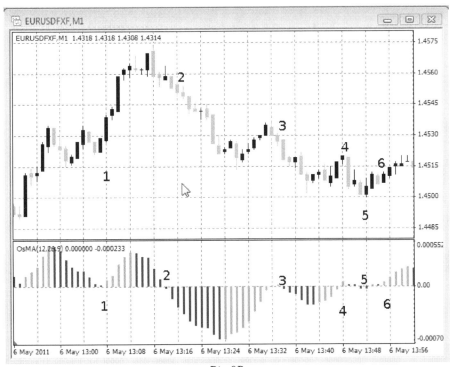

Pic 9B

Trade #1 on the above chart demonstrates a situation that can and does occur with some frequency. You can tell from the downward slope of the OSMA bars starting just prior to 13:00 that price is moving down and that a Sell trade is likely to be signaled in the next few minutes.

However, as you can see at #1 above, price rallied and the OSMA bars began to start moving back up, without ever once crossing and closing below the zero line. This is just as valid a signal as if the bars crossed and closed over the zero line for the first time. You may go days without seeing this happen, and you might see it happen more than once during a single session (as we do here at both #1 and #3).

Trades #4 and #5 also demonstrate something important. Sometimes this method gives you a (GASP!) losing trade. Here we racked up 2 losers in a row for 10 pips each.

4 winning trades x 5 pips = +20
2 losing trades x 10 pips = -20

Net for this session: 0 pips.

Some days (or sessions) just turn out this way. It really is NO BIG DEAL!

No one wins every trade. NO ONE! Get used to losing a trade now and then because it's going to happen no matter how hard you work or how much you pray. As long as you are using solid money management, losses should never be a big deal. You just shake them off and keep moving forward.

Pic 9C

Trade #3 went nowhere fast and cost us 10 pips, but the other 4 trades netted 5 apiece.

4 winners x 5 pips = +20 pips
1 loser x 10 pips = -10 pips.

Net gain for the session: +10 pips.

For the day: +35 pips (25 +10 + 0 = 35 pips).

How fast would you be quitting your real job if you were knocking out 35 pips gains on a daily basis?

Sensible Forex

That's a rhetorical question...don't answer it. My point is, there are some very simple trading methods out there that if you stick with them, you're going to end up making money as a Forex trader.

All you have to do is make up your mind you're going to stick with one of them and actually start placing trades.

Real money trades.

The rest will pretty much take care of itself.

Chapter Ten

Mrs. Watanabe's Secret

Part 1

In a small house in the Gohongi suburb of Tokyo, an alarm starts to ring. It's 4:55 a.m., and Mrs. Watanabe reaches over quickly to silence it. Her husband is still asleep, having arrived home from work just a few hours earlier, and Mrs. Watanabe wants him to get another 30 minutes of sleep before he must head back to his job as a salaryman.

Mrs. Watanabe gently slides from her bed and walks down the

hallway into the kitchen. This is where she begins her day; turning on the hot water kettle to make tea, getting the rice cooker ready for another day; cutting up some fresh fruit she picked up at the market yesterday afternoon, and so forth.

By the time she is done, she can hear Mr. Watanabe starting to stir in the bedroom. And in the room across the hall, she can hear the faint sounds of the latest pop group's hit new song as her daughter's clock radio alarm goes off. It won't be long before the entire family joins Mrs. Watanabe around the table for breakfast.

The next hour rushes by, as her daughter and her husband get ready to start their days. Mr. Watanabe works for an accounting firm in Tokyo, and must ride 3 different trains to reach his office. This means he has to be out the front door no later than 6:10 a.m. if he wants to get to work on time.

And in Japan, EVERYONE wants to get to work on time. Tardiness is not tolerated.

Her daughter is also in a rush to get out of the house. Her friends will be at her door shortly, and they will walk to school together. Even though the school is more than 3 miles from the Watanabe home, Mrs. Watanabe is not worried about her daughter. Crime against children is almost non-existent in Japan, and she has her friends with her for "group protection." Even on days when it is raining, the kids prefer to walk and enjoy each other's company, rather than take a 5 minute ride in a car to get to school dry.

By 7 a.m. the house is quiet, and Mrs. Watanabe now turns to her daily household chores: cleaning up after her family. With her TV on in the background, tuned into one of the daily news and entertainment shows, she wipes, sweeps, mops and cleans her home from top to bottom. She even finds time to get a couple of loads of laundry done.

Sensible Forex

Even though she spends several hours each day on housecleaning, Mrs. Watanabe does not mind. Having a clean home for her family to enjoy and her friends to visit is one of her top priorities.

Early in the afternoon, Mrs. Watanabe heads out to the local supermarket to buy what she needs to make dinner for herself and her daughter. Her husband will be out late again tonight, socializing with his friends from work. Mrs. Watanabe does not mind, simply because this is how things are done in Japan. The husband works hard all week, and social norms require him to spend time after work eating and drinking with co-workers and clients.

As Mrs. Watanabe browses the enormous selections of fruits, vegetables and meat, she can't help but notice that prices have risen dramatically in the last few weeks. At first she begins to do the math in her head, calculating how much she can afford to spend on this one meal.

Then Mrs. Watanabe stops, and smiles to herself. "I am so *baka*[1]" she thinks. Old habits surely do die hard.

Because the truth of the matter is that Mrs. Watanabe could easily afford anything and everything in the store if that's how she wanted to spend her money.

She selects some thinly cut Kobe Beef and a variety of vegetables so that she can make "shabu-shabu" for her and her daughter. On her way out of the store she notices that the bakery has some new cakes on display, including one shaped and frosted to look exactly like a panda bear. Knowing her daughter loves pandas, Mrs. Watanabe spends the $65 and buys her daughter the small panda "cake for one."

---

[1] "baka" is Japanese for "stupid" or "foolish"

Sensible Forex

Knowing her daughter will be out of school soon, Mrs. Watanabe exits the store and returns home to begin preparing for dinner. Her daughter is delighted to see the Panda cake, but is hesitant to eat it simply because "it's so kawaii[2]!!!!!"

Mrs. Watanabe cleans up after dinner, washing the dishes and putting them into the strainer to dry. Her daughter is already taking a bath, so Mrs. Watanabe sits down to watch a game show on TV until her daughter is out of the bathroom. Then it's Mrs. Watanabe's turn for a nice, relaxing hot bath. She enjoys soaking in the hot water, and can feel her muscles relaxing to the point she nearly falls asleep in the tub.

After her bath, Mrs. Watanabe and her daughter sit in the living room and sip cups of hot tea, watching the latest Korean drama on TV. By 10 p.m. her daughter is sleepy and heads upstairs for bed. But not Mrs. Watanabe.

Mrs. Watanabe heads into her small "office" which is really just a corner in her bedroom. She turns on her computer and opens the trading platform provided by her Forex broker. At exactly 10:30 p.m., she checks her charts, sees that her indicators are telling her to "sell the EUR/JPY" and she does just that…she enters a Sell Contract on the Euro / Japanese Yen. Over the course of the next 30 minutes, she sees that the Euro is indeed falling in value against the Yen, and when her position reaches +20 pips, she closes out the trade and then goes to sleep.

Another $20,000 richer.

Before continuing, there are two things you need to know about Mrs.

---

[2] "kawaii" is Japanese for "cute"

Sensible Forex

Watanabe:

1. Mrs. Watanabe does not exist; and yet
2. Mrs. Watanabe is very, very real.

Are you totally confused? Let me explain.

The "Mrs. Watanabe" of our story is not a real person in the sense that no one by that name was interviewed for this project.

But "Mrs. Watanabe" is very real. Mrs. Watanabe is a composite of hundreds of thousands of Japanese housewives who live their daily lives in much the same fashion as was described for our Mrs. Watanabe. They are married, have one or more children who are in school, and spend the bulk of their day dealing with household chores like cooking, cleaning, shopping and helping their children.

But when 10:30 p.m. rolls around, they drop what they are doing and transform into Forex Trading Machines!

It's estimated that more than one million Japanese housewives are online trading Forex between the hours of 10 p.m. and midnight, Monday through Friday of each week.

It's also estimated that more than two hundred thousand Japanese housewives have built up trading accounts in excess of One Million Dollars over the last 5+ years.

None of these women brought any sort of special skills to the table. They had no formal education in finance, and many have no education beyond a high school diploma. They married young, started a family, and have relied upon their husbands to be the sole breadwinner in the family.

Sensible Forex

But after years of economic malaise in Japan, they realized that in order to build a brighter future for their families and themselves, they were going to be required to find an additional source of income to help handle rising family bills and still be able to add to their retirement accounts.

At first, most of these women turned to the stock market to find vehicles for financial growth. In the late 1980's (prior to the spread of the personal computer) it was not unusual for a Japanese family to have a stock "ticker" on a shelf somewhere, which would print out a constant stream of price information on various company shares when the Nikkei (Japanese stock market) was open for business.

But far too many women were wiped out (and more than once in many cases) when the bottom fell out of the Nikkei Index (the Japanese version of the Dow Jones). It happened several times over the course of twenty years...the Index would rise as stocks got stronger, and then in the course of just a few hours, prices would crash and traders would find their positions wiped out.

It was the advent of retail Forex trading that changed the world for these Samurai Traders.

Once trading rules were changed to allow small traders into Currency Trading, the one million + Mrs. Watanabes swung into action. They took classes to educate themselves on how the Forex markets worked, and they studied the various accepted methods of trading which seemed to hold the most promise.

There were some false starts along the way, and plenty of women lost their entire trading accounts due to some questionable practices on both their part and their brokers.

But as time went on, several Mrs. Watanabes started to make some real money trading Forex. At first, this handful of traders kept their mouths shut and their eyes open, fine tuning a trading method that started out showing great promise, and just kept getting better as the months passed.

What stated out as a small group of winning traders began to grow, as one Mrs. Watanabe would share her secret with a sister, or mother, or close friend. As those Mrs. Watanabe's began to experience success, they too shared "the secret" with one or two women close to them.

And like that old shampoo commercial from years ago once said, they told two friends, and so on, and so on, and so on...

Fast forward to today and there are now more than one million Japanese housewives who have built up 5-7 figure trading accounts, placing no more than 2-3 trades a day in most cases, and limiting their trading time to just a couple of hours, late at night.

They don't have a set of charts cluttered with a dozen indicators.

They don't run EA's (robots) that do the trading for them...in fact, most of them never heard of the terms "EA" or "robot" as they are used in trading.

Most importantly, they don't spend hours a day staring at charts, trying to decipher what is happening in the markets on a minute-by-minute basis.

They sit down in front of their charts at the same time every night. They look for their trade setups, which appear nearly every night, and on multiple pairs. They place their trades, and either watch the charts until they've made their money, or place stop loss and profit target trades to automatically execute once a certain price is reached, and they go to bed.

Sensible Forex

The Mrs. Watanabes of Japan do not have a lot of free time. Between getting their husband and children ready for work and school, and keeping their house running in an orderly fashion, there just isn't a lot of time left for them to spend in any other ventures.

That's why it's important to them to use a trading method that not only has a high winning percentage, but it must not take more than an hour or two of their precious free time.

This is what motivated the original Mrs. Watanabes to find the method that is so popular amongst Japanese housewives.

And the fact that there are thousands upon thousands of Japanese families worth more than a million dollars, where there is only one person in the family working (and only earning a moderate wage to boot) is proof of the effectiveness of that trading method.

So would you like to know how Mrs. Watanabe (all one million of her) made a fortune in Forex?

It boils down to three factors:

1. Trading at the same time every day
2. Using moderately aggressive money management
3. Using a trading method with a proven high probability of success

That's really all it boils down to. And in this chapter, I'm going to cover #1 thoroughly. In the next chapter I'll show you exactly how Mrs. Watanabe allows the miracle of "compounding" to turn her small stake ($1,000) into seven figures in less than 12 months.

And finally, in Part #3 I'll discuss the trading method Mrs. Watanabe uses to find trades setups that allow her to make her pip target nearly every trading day.

For now, though, let's look at factor #1—Trading at the same time every day.

In the story above, I told you how Mrs. Watanabe doesn't even turn on her computer or look at her charts until 10 p.m. (usually right before 10:30).

That's 10:30 p.m. in Japan, which is 13-14 hours ahead of the Eastern United States (depending on whether we are in Daylight Savings Time or Standard Time).

But when we roll our clocks ahead or behind an hour, Mrs. Watanabe is the one who has to adjust her trading time.

In the U.S., the starting time is ALWAYS the same: 9:30 a.m. eastern time.

Would you care to hazard a guess as to why that time is so important?

I won't keep you in suspense: 9:30 a.m. eastern time is when the U.S. stock markets open for business.

And several years ago Mrs. Watanabe discovered something about the correlation between currency prices and the opening of the U.S. stock markets: On most days (4 out of 5 days on average) currency prices on the major pairs will make a decent sized move (25-100 pips) normally within the first hour after the stock market opens for business.

Sometimes this move is a continuation of price movement that began hours earlier.

Sensible Forex

Sometimes that move is a reversal of the price action that has been hours long in the making.

But on most trading days, between 9:30 a.m. and 10:30 a.m. eastern time, you see a significant run up (or run down) in the price of the major pairs.

And this is what Mrs. Watanabe is targeting. She knows that for an hour or so of her time invested, she is going to see enough price action take place that she can confidently place a trade, make her targeted number of pips (more on that in a bit), and get out of the market, her money safely returned to her trading account.

Most Forex "experts" would agree with Mrs. Watanabe's focus on a specific time period, even though 99% have never thought to time their entry into a Forex trade with the opening of the U.S. stock market.

Instead, most focus on the "opening" of the three major currency trading centers: London (3 a.m. eastern), New York (8 a.m. eastern) and Asia (6/7 p.m. eastern).

And while there is definitely an increase of activity around these times, too often that activity involves quickly spiking prices, which tend to work against as many trades as they benefit.

Further, at least in the case of the London open, the major price movements can take place in the 3 hour period leading up to the London open, which then can leave prices flat for several hours afterwards. There rarely is any rhyme or reason as to when those "early" movements will take place, so traders either have to adjust their schedule and spend more time in front of their charts (4-6 hours a day) or simply miss out on the early price movement and hope that

184

there is enough momentum left over after 3 a.m. that they can "make their pips."

But remember, Mrs. Watanabe is a busy woman, and she doesn't have time to sit in front of her charts all day and all night. She just wants to get in, get paid, and get out.

So through a long and costly process of trial and error, she knows to limit her trading to the hours between 10:30 p.m. and midnight. This is where her trading method has the highest rate of return.

In the next chapter, I'll discuss the actual style of Money Management Mrs. Watanabe employs while trading.

But just to give you a small taste right now, Mrs. Watanabe only wants to make 20 pips a day. Sometimes she makes more, but she will not settle for less if she can avoid it.

And based on "diet" a 20 pips a day, Mrs. Watanabe could turn a $1,000 trading account into 7 figures in as little as 191 trading days (which works out to about 8-1/2 months, using 22 trading days a month as a constant). It could happen a little sooner if she consistently makes more pips each day, or it can take longer if she fails to hit her target consistently.

But suffice to say, Mrs. Watanabe eventually makes her pips and gets paid.

And if you follow her advice, you'll do the same.

Mrs. Watanabe's Secret
Part 2

Before jumping in, let's just quickly review the important points from Part 1 of Mrs. Watanabe's Secret.

Mrs. Watanabe is a busy woman, who can't afford to spend 4-6 hours a day staring at the charts on her screen. She needs to be able to get into and out of a trade with a reasonable profit, and do so inside of a couple of hours. So she trades starting at 10:30 at night (her time, in Japan) and she shoots for 20 pips profit. When she gets 20 pips, she closes out her trade and goes to bed. And her 20 pips of profit has a dollar value of $20,000 (meaning she is trading 100 lots x $10 per pip = $1,000 per pip, so 20 pips equals $20,000).

If she were trading 50 full lots, her pip value would be 50 lots x $10 per pip = $500 per pip, and a 20 pip gain would equal $10,000.

Another way of stating that would be 1 standard lot has a pip value of $10 (1 x $10 = $10). 2 standard lots would have a pip value of $20 (2 x $10 = $20). 10 lots would have a pip value of $100 (10 x $10 = $100). And so on.

The concepts behind Mrs. Watanabe's success are simple: she uses a moderately aggressive style of Money Management, and she allows the "power of compounding" to grow her account into 7 figures at warp speed.

Most of you are probably familiar with the riddle about the Penny versus the $20 Bill. If not, here is a quick recitation:

A young man asks his grandfather to pay him for raking the leaves up from the older man's lawn. The grandfather agrees, but tells the younger man he will give him a choice in how he is to be paid: he can either take $20 right now, or he can agree to work for one penny today, with the promise that the old man will double that amount the next day ($.02) and continue to double the daily balance for 30 consecutive days, at which point the young man can come by and pick up his earnings.

If the young man agrees to accept the $20, then he has earned a grand total of $20 for his efforts,

If the young man agrees to accept the value of a penny, doubled every day for 30 consecutive days, the young man will earn $5,368,709.12.

And that is the power of compounding.

You take your base amount, you add in the earnings you made on that base amount, and now have a new base amount on which to earn even more.

If you have an investment that pays 10% per year, and you allow your 10% earnings to remain in that investment (forcing the 10% calculation to be made in succeeding years on a larger base amount) it will take you about 7.2 years to double your money.

If you want to play with this idea, you need to know about the Rule of 72.

The Rule of 72 says "Take the number 72 and divide it by your expected interest rate to get the period of time it will take you to double your money."

So if you are expecting 10%, you divide 72 by .10 and get 7.2 year. If you are expecting a 20% interest rate, you divide 72 by .20 and get 3.6 years. And so on.

Sensible Forex

The thing about Forex is, you don't need to limit yourself to 10% earnings and take 7+ years to double your account. In fact, if you follow the charts I've included in this second part and take them out to 7 years, you're going to find that your projected earnings (which you will NEVER reach, I promise you) are equal to about 2500 times the actual amount of total wealth here on the planet.

In other words, at some point you hit a wall and can go no further, even though on paper you still show lots of room for growth.

But that's the power of compounding.

If you have the ability to leave your earnings in your account, and use those earnings to increase the size of your trades proportionally, in a very short period of time you are going to be earning more money in a single trade than most people make in a full year of employment.

So let's talk about how aggressive Mrs. Watanabe is when she is trading.

In all of the examples I'm about to give you, assume that the trader started with $1,000 in their account.

A trader who wanted to be **ultra-conservative** would never trade full lots ($10/pip), or even mini-lots ($1/pip) with only $1,000 to start. Instead, they would trade what are called micro-lots, where the pip value can range from $.01 to $.10 (that's one penny to one dime).

Assuming the trader's micro-lot was worth one penny, and the account had $1,000 in it, the trader could lose 100,000 pips before they lost their entire account.

While this probably sound attractive from a loss standpoint, you have to realize that when your gains are measured in pennies, it could literally take years before the trader was able to double that account from $1,000 to $2,000 (I haven't done the math, but my gut instinct tells me it would take a year or two, at a minimum, assuming the trader hit their 20 pip target every day).

There is nothing wrong with a "slow and steady" approach, but if it took only 2 years to double the account, it would take 14-15 years before the account even reached 6 figures.

That might be fine for some people, but Mrs. Watanabe does not have that kind of time to wait.

If the micro-lots were valued at $.10 a pip, Mrs. Watanabe would start out by making $2 a day (20 pips x $.10 = $2.00) and her rate of growth in her account would certainly be much quicker than it would be using one penny lots. But again, the time it would take to double the account from $1,000 to $2,000 would be approximately 2-1/2 years.

Assuming a consistent rate of growth, she would see 6 figures in about 10 years, which again would be fine for a lot of traders (and a whole lot more than in the first example).

But even that rate of growth is too slow for Mrs. Watanabe.

She is looking for a way to get into the 6-7 figure range quickly (meaning much faster than 10 years from now) but at the same time, not be in a position where she puts her entire account at risk on any one trade.

But before I get into the nuts and bolts of how she trades, let's look at the other end of the spectrum…what I like to call the Stone Drunk Las Vegas Style of Money Management.

Sensible Forex

Instead of trading micro-lots on a $1,000 account, the S.D.L.V.S. of M.M. calls for the trader to place as large a trade as his broker will allow with a $1,000 account.

Since most brokers offer 100-1 leverage for these trades[3], a $1,000 account would allow a trader to place as much as 1 Full Lot into action, where the pip value is $10. That means the trader has only a 100 pip cushion between himself and a total account wipeout (100 pips x $10 = $1,000).

That simply does not leave much room for error.

Even worse are the brokers who offer 200-1 leverage. This allows the crazy trader to place as much as 2 Full Lots into play, where the pip value is $20. Now the trader is down to a 50 pip cushion (50 pips x $20 = $1,000).

Anyone who has traded Forex in the past knows that it doesn't exactly take an event of earth shattering importance to get the markets to move 50 pips in the wrong direction very, very quickly. If this should happen to our Las Vegas trader, and he is working without a stop-loss in place, he could see his entire $1,000 disappear in a matter of minutes (possibly even seconds).

This kind of risk is entirely unacceptable to Mrs. Watanabe, and she would never trade in such a fashion simply because the risk does not justify the reward.

So how exactly does Mrs. Watanabe trade?

---

[3] Since this report was written, the NFA and CFTC have acted to limit trader accounts in the USA to 50-1, thus denying traders the opportunity to blow their accounts up as quickly as they might with 100-1 leverage or higher.

Sensible Forex

She trades using mini-lots, but where conservative traders would only trade using 1 mini lot for every $1,000 in their account, Mrs. Watanabe trades 1 mini lot for every $500 in her account.

1 mini-lot per $1,000 is considered to be conservative, particularly if you are using a 20 pip stop loss, so that a 20 pip (or $20) loss would only equal 2% of your over all account. An overall risk of 2-3% of your account on any one trade is considered to be well within reason.

As for Mrs. Watanabe, she is actually putting a maximum of 4% of her account at risk (trading with a 20 pip stop-loss). The word "maximum" is used here because in many of her trades, while she sets a 20 pip stop loss, when the trade moves against her (meaning a buy signal turns into a sell signal, and vice versa) she will manually exit the trade when the current price has not yet triggered her stop loss order.

And rather than waiting 1-1/2 to 10 years to see her $1,000 account double into $2,000, Mrs. Watanabe follows a strict trading plan that allows her the opportunity to double her account in as little as 22 trading days (which works out to being 1 month, assuming there are 22 trading days in one month).

She trades at the same time every night, shoots for 20 pips profit (which can come in 1, 2 or even 3 separate trades, depending on how the market is acting at the time) and closes down her platform for the night once she hits her target.

People who are not familiar with Forex just can't seem to accept that it really is just that easy to make a fortune, starting with an amount that is less than the average house payment in America.

But for anyone who has the patience and the discipline to follow a very simple trading plan, and trade using a very simple set of rules, these kinds of profits not only are possible, they are actually being made every day (or night) in households all over Japan, and the rest of the world as well.

Earlier you read about the power of compounding, and how fast you could turn a penny into multiple millions of dollars, just by doubling it once a day.

We aren't doubling accounts once a day, so it will take a longer period of time to see a million dollars in your trading account.

But not that much longer.

And to prove it, here is a chart showing exactly how much money you would need to make every day, trading Forex, to turn your $1,000 account into $1,000,000.00.

∧∧∧∧∧∧∧∧∧∧∧∧∧∧∧∧∧∧∧

(Editor's Note: The charts intended for this section have been reproduced on pages 28 through 34 of this book)

Assuming 22 trading days a month, it would take between 8 and 9 months to turn a $1,000 account into 7 figures (also assuming you traded each day until you reached your 20 pip goal, and further assuming there were no substantial breaks taken, such as Thanksgiving, Christmas/New Year and the month of August, all of which are generally considered to be poor times to trade).

Factoring in those times of poor trading (plus about a dozen or so national holidays when banks are closed and trading volume is between low and non-existent), following this 20 Pip Stair Step Method would take the average trader around 1 year to reach 7 figures, again assuming a starting balance of $1,000.

I know I'm repeating myself here, but these are points worth repeating. You are talking about trading for 1-1/2 hours (2 hours tops) and looking for certain trade setups that occur routinely (4 out of 5 days a week, on average). You place anywhere from 1-3 trades, and in the case of 3 trades, you are looking to make 6-8 pips per trade (or whatever combination works out to 20 pips profit).

If you will just follow the rules of the trading method and stick to this trading plan, there is almost no way you can fail to make 7 figures in a year.

Almost no way.

I say "almost" because you have to allow for those unforeseen circumstances that can temporarily derail any good plan. For instance, I once lost about 80 pips on a trade because I sent the trade in, saw that it was executed, but before I could place stop loss and limit orders, I lost power at my house. My options were to either wait for the power to come back on and then place the secondary trades, or call my broker and ask them to place them manually for me.

And since I kept my broker's phone number in a file **online**…

I was stuck in limbo for almost 2 hours before power was restored and I signed back in, only to see I was down 80 pips on the trade. I took the loss, and then went to my broker's website and wrote down the phone number in about a half dozen different places around my house so I would always have access to the number in case a similar instance should ever occur.

But assuming you don't suffer from power brownouts on a regular basis, or your cable modem doesn't crap out on you for no apparent reason (another problem I've had, but thankfully haven't lost any money as a result) or who knows what, then you should be able to follow this trade plan and start building the kind of trading account most people will not even have the courage to dream about.

And some of you might even be in a position to get there faster.

Mrs. Watanabe spends very little time in front of her charts. And frankly, she tends to trade the EUR/USD, USD/JPY and EUR/JPY as her primary pairs. The reason for this is that (1) The EUR/USD has a strong tendency to make a 20 pip move starting immediately after the close of the 9:30 candle (using 5 minute charts) (2) the USD/JPY is a pair that normally moves 5-15 pips in one direction at a time, making it simple to get about half of her daily pip requirements in one trade and (3) the EUR/JPY tends to move 10-25 pips in one direction at a time, making it simple to earn her entire 20 pip goal in one trade. If she has already made 5-10 pips on a EUR/USD or USD/JPY trade, all she needs is another 10-15 pips on the EUR/JPY and she can usually get that without even breaking a sweat.

But maybe you have a little more time than Mrs. Watanabe. Or maybe you don't mind trading pairs that are a little more volatile than the three Mrs. Watanabe trades. Maybe a 20 pip goal is too easy for you, and you know that with the right trading method, you could easily make more in one day.

If this describes you, then pay attention to this next Stair Step. It makes the same assumption in terms of starting account size, and it follows Mrs. Watanabe's rule of trading 1 mini-lot per $500 in the account.

But instead of shooting for 20 pips a day, this Stair Step assumes a daily goal of 40 pips.

And look at the difference in the speed at which your account could grow using this set of parameters.

(Editor's Note: The charts intended for this section have been reproduced on pages 34 through 37 of this book)

Assuming 22 trading days a month, you could reach $1 Million in as little as 4-1/2 months.

You'll notice a couple of differences between these two Stair Steps.

First would be the time it takes to reach 7 figures. By increasing your daily goal to 40 pips, you could reach seven figures in as little as 98 trading days, which works out to 4-1/2 months. Using a 20 pip goal took you twice as long (around 9 months under optimal conditions).

Another difference you might have noticed is that this Stair Step quits using mini lots after you reach $25,000 (5 full lots). I set it up this way simply because trading with a combination of full and mini-lots is a pain and requires you to make constant adjustments to your trading platform. By switching to full lots early on, it simplifies your trading a bit.

But if you wanted to keep adding mini-lots onto your trades to stick with a very strict 1 mini-lot per $500 in the account rule, you could do so for as long as you like, and hit your 7 figure target that much faster.

The last thing you might have noticed about both Stair Steps is that at a later point in each, your trade size reached 100 lots and never went beyond that level.

The reason I drew it up this way is that most major Forex brokers will guarantee instant fills on any trade size of 100 lots or smaller. If you go beyond 100 lots (to 101 lots or more) you could run into trouble getting your trade filled, meaning you might find yourself getting a worse entry price than you would had your order been no more than 100 lots. Poor entry prices usually end up equaling poor trades, and should be avoided at all costs.

And since you are already in sniffing distance of seven figures when you get to the 100 lot trade size, it really doesn't take that much longer to reach your goal than you would if you continually increased your trade size in accordance with the 1 mini-lot per $500 rule.

So now you know the second component to Mrs. Watanabe's Secret...how she structures each trade to get maximum value for each pip while at the same time not putting too much of her account at risk on any one trade.

There is only one piece of the puzzle left to be put into place...Mrs. Watanabe's Trading Method. And we'll go over that method in detail in the next chapter.

Mrs. Watanabe's Secret
Part 3

In the previous two sections, you've learned how Mrs. Watanabe has turned herself into a Forex Trading Machine, trading at the same time every day, and shooting for a very reasonable number of pips in each trading session, while being only somewhat aggressive in her money management, and never risking more than 4% of her trading account on any one trade.

In this last report, we'll look at exactly how Mrs. Watanabe finds the kinds of trades that consistently earn her 20 pips per trading session.

In order to take full advantage of Mrs. Watanabe's Trading Method, you are going to need to open an account with a Forex Broker that offers MT4 charts. It won't be a problem finding one, since there are more than 100 of them out there, spread all around the world.

Once you have the platform installed and operating on your computer, your next step will be to install some "custom" indicators that Mrs. Watanabe uses in her trading. Specifically, you'll be installing the Slope Direction Line, the SignalAM and the OsMA.

In the Appendix of this book I'll tell you exactly where you can get access to those indicators if you do not already have them installed in your MT4 Platform.

In trading Forex pairs, Mrs. Watanabe concentrates on the Five (5) Minute Charts. She has found that the One (1) Minute Charts are just too erratic for her taste, and the Fifteen (15) Minute Charts are just too slow in setting up new trades for the time period she's chosen. So almost by default, she ended up on the 5 minute Charts.

But don't let my use of the word "default" discount the value of the 5 Minute Charts. Because these charts move faster than the 15 Minute Charts (meaning you see 3 candles on the 5 minute chart where you only see one candle on the 15 minute chart) traders simply get more chances to find entry and exit points for their trades. Where you might get 2 trade signals on a 15 Minute Chart, you could easily get 5 or 6 signals on a 5 Minute Chart for the same pair.

And since Mrs. Watanabe is only looking for 20 pips total for a single trading session, and she is willing to place as many as 3 trades to get there, using the 5 minute charts means she could find as many as 10-15 trade opportunities in the 1-2 hours she is online, just by using the 5 minute charts.

As for the charts themselves, it really doesn't matter if you use a Bar Chart or Candlesticks. Mrs. Watanabe prefers candlesticks, and the fact that they used to be commonly referred to as "Japanese candlesticks" before the name was shortened down to "candlesticks" might have something to do with her choice. The "candlestick" method of charting commodity prices has been a staple of Japanese traders for hundreds of years.

But don't feel like you are wedded to tradition. If you find you prefer using Bar charts, go right ahead. Since you are entering when a new 5 minute candle/bar opens, it really makes no difference which you use.

Once you've made your bar/candlestick decision, your next step is to install the indicators on your chart.

As was mentioned in one of the earlier chapters of this report, Mrs. Watanabe focuses her attention on three trading pairs: the EUR/USD, EUR/JPY and USD/JPY. You should open all three of these pairs on your platform (one of the earlier referenced videos shows you exactly how to do that).

You install three indicators on your charts: the OsMA; the Slope Direction Line; and the SignalAM indicator. You'll find download links for all three indicators in the Appendix to this book.

Once you have all of your indicators in place, your chart should look something like this:

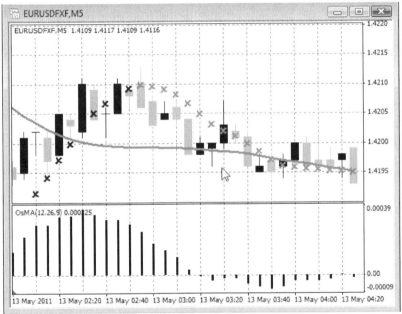

Pic 10-1

As I noted earlier, I use the "factory" settings for the OsMA and the SignalAM. For the Slope Direction Line, I adjust the Inputs Values to 34,2,0 and change the colors to Lime Green for Upward Trends and Magenta for Downward Trends. This helps the Slope Line stand out against the rest of the chart.

Sensible Forex

You, of course, are free to choose any two colors you like. Just make sure you can see all the different indicators clearly.

And now the good part: how to use these indicators to spot trades that will allow you to consistently earn 20 pips per day.

As is noted repeatedly throughout these reports, you don't start trading until 9:30 a.m. eastern time. But you should have your charts open and loaded a few minutes before that, just to make sure you don't have any connection issues. It also gives you a chance to get a feel for what the market has been doing for the last several hours, and after some time, you will be able to predict with some accuracy what the pairs are likely to do over the next couple of hours.

When she is ready to trade, what Mrs. Watanabe is looking for is (1) The overall current trend of the pairs on the 5 Minute Charts, as represented by the Slope Direction Line, (2) the Overall current strength of the trend, as represented by the OsMA, and (3) an entry point for her trade, as represented by the SignalAM.

So let's break down each step into bite-size pieces.

1. The Slope Direction Line is a great tool to use to spot the overall trend in the market (the trend being Up or Down). As I'll show in my illustrations, I use a Lime Green Slope Direction Line to indicate the overall trend is Up, which means if I want to trade the pair, I would look to BUY the pair. The Magenta Slope Direction Line indicates a Downward Trend, which means I will be looking to SELL that pair if I decide to place a trade.

One thing to remember about the Slope Direction Line is that when you see a color change take place, that change can be "erased" and the original color be put back in place if the price of the pair resumes the previous direction (otherwise known as "repainting"). I know that's confusing, so let me give you an example...

If price has been moving downward for several hours, my Slope Line will be Magenta colored. This tells me the current overall trend in Down. Price can level off for a while and even begin to move upward a bit. At some point, the Slope Line will turn Lime Green, indicating the overall trend is now up.

However, if price makes an immediate reversal and starts heading down again, it can "erase" the Lime Green color and reinstate the Magenta color, and if you were not watching the pairs when that happened, you would probably never know that the Slope Line gave out a signal that turned out to be false.

As a further However, however, when you start trading at 9:30 a.m. eastern time, you will rarely see the Slope Line repaint. The reason for this is there is normally a market direction which is set at 8:00 a.m. when the east coast banks open and begin trading. On most mornings, financial reports are released at 8:30 a.m., and the 8:00 a.m. trend is either strengthened, or abruptly reversed, all depending on the level of good (or bad) news contained in that report.

But by 9:30 a.m., the original trend from the 8:00 a.m. opening has usually run its course, and a reversal of that trend begins to form. It does not necessarily start immediately at 9:30...it can take until 10, or even 10:30 (and sometimes later than that) for the trend reversal to start taking shape.

But once the trend starts to reverse and the Slope Line changes color, it is a very safe bet that the new trend will continue for some time, giving Mrs. Watanabe a very good chance of making 10-20 pips on one trade.

2. The OsMA Indicator—OsMA is shorthand for Oscillator of Moving Averages, and frankly, any further explanation is going to get into some pretty deep territory, which is not the idea here. If you want to know all the gory details on how the OsMA is composed and what it represents, just do a Google search on "OsMA indicator" and you'll get dozens of sites that purport to explain the indicator in excruciating detail.

What you need to know about the OsMA is that it does a very good job of detecting trends and trend changes. You can see in the chart capture below the series of lines that form waves (or mounds, or half circles, or whatever description best suits you). When a trend begins to falter, the OsMA will begin to head in the opposite direction.

What I mean by this is that the lines that form the OsMA move up or down, form some peaks that may consist of one or more lines that touch a high (or low) point, and then begin to shrink down and head in the opposite direction. Once those lines begin to head in the opposite direction, you know that a new trend is about to begin.

It may take a few (or a lot) of candles for that new trend to materialize, but in almost all cases, price will ultimately reverse its current course and start trending in the opposite direction.

Mrs. Watanabe uses the OsMA as a form of "confirmation" that the signals she is getting from the other indicators are in fact "good signals" and that she now has a high probability of making her 20 pips by following those signals and placing the appropriate trade.

3. The SignalAM Indicator—The SignalAM is an interesting item. It was originally developed to be used on longer term charts (1 hour and 4 hour) where it has a remarkable ability to "signal" trend changes several hours before the actual trend starts to materialize. In a flat market, this can mean getting into a trade 20-100 pips earlier than

anyone else in the market who is relying upon other more popular indicators for their signals.

And truthfully, if used alone, the SignalAM is just too flaky an indicator to use on shorter term charts. Yes, it will spot trend reversals early and allow a trader to get into a trade at the earliest point possible.

But it will also give off countless "false alarms" that will constantly leave traders 5-20 pips upside down on a trade when a new competing signal is given in the opposite direction. A lot of testing was done with the SignalAM on the short term charts, and a warning was given out to users to stick with the 1 and 4 hour charts when using this indicator.

However, some additional tests were run using the SignalAm in conjunction with other indicators, to see how each worked both independently and as part of a team. It was during these tests that an amazing discovery was made:

When you combined the SignalAM with the Slope Direction Line, and only traded in the direction indicated by the Slope, you now had a way of discounting the bad signals given off by the SignalAM and routinely getting excellent entry points for trades moving in the same direction as the Slope Line.

^^^^^^^^^^^^^^^^^^^^^^^

Now let me make this one point very, very clear: Mrs. Watanabe does NOT trade using the Slope Direction Line OR the SignalAM...the reason for this is she uses a Japan-based broker that does NOT offer the MT4 platform that we use here in the West.

HOWEVER, she DOES use two indicators that are virtually

IDENTICAL to the Slope and the SignalAM, so what you are seeing when you use these two indicators on your MT4 platform is more or less exactly what Mrs. Watanabe is seeing on HER platform as well.

But getting back to the actual trading, using these indicators, Mrs. Watanabe is looking for one of two things: Either a new trend which develops at or after 9:30 a.m. eastern time, or an existing trend getting stronger after 9:30 a.m.

A new trend developing is very easy to spot. Prior to 9:30 a.m., you should see a series of candles moving in one direction for a period of time (normally starting between 8-8:30 a.m., but sometimes even earlier). As 9:30 approaches, price begins to flatten out, and you begin to see prices staying within a defined range (usually 10-15 pips). At or after 9:30 a.m., both the SignalAm and the Slope line change color, indicating a new trend is developing. A quick glance at the OsMA should give a concurring signal: either the bars of the OsMA are shrinking towards the new trend, or they have broken through the "zero line" and are now also moving in the direction of the trend.

An existing trend is a little tougher to spot, and relies heavily on both the OsMA and the SignalAM. As noted previously, is the bars of the OsMA are shrinking in the opposite direction of the existing trade, this indicates the trend is getting weaker, and the best bet is to wait for a new trend to develop and enter your trade then.

But there are times when the OsMA is shrinking back towards the zero line, but begins to regain strength and starts to grow away from zero, indicating the trend is getting stronger. When you see that starting to happen, it's a clear sign that the trend is going to continue for a while.

So your next step would be to consult the SignalAM. When a trend starts to die off, you usually get a "reverse signal" or a signal to trade in the opposite direction, long before either the Slope Line or the OsMA starts to give off signals that the trend is resuming.

So in many, if not most cases, the SignalAM is going to be giving an opposite signal for another candle or two. As long as the Slope Line is still showing the original signal direction, and the OsMA is now showing a resumption of the trend, you wait for SignalAM to give a new signal which is in accord with the other two indicators, and you place your trade at that time.

Just to be 100% transparent, there is technically a third chart setup which does occur from time to time at 9:30 a.m., but it is really not so much of a setup as it is chart chaos.

What I'm talking about is those times where the OsMA is almost completely flat and both the Slope and the SignalAM keep switching back and forth between Buy and Sell signals. These times are easy to spot simply because you can see in the previous few candles prior to 9:30 a.m. that there have been 2-3 competing signals given out by the indicators.

What that means to Mrs. Watanabe is to simply be patient, and wait for a trend to develop. It may take 30 minutes, or an hour, but almost always a discernable trend begins to take shape, and Mrs. Watanabe trades it accordingly.

And on those rare days when NO trend takes shape, what does Mrs. Watanabe do?

She goes to bed without placing ANY trades.

After all, you can't lose what you do not risk, and why risk a single penny if there is no clear trend to follow?

Mrs. Watanabe is patient and is willing to skip a trading day, simply because she knows that a tradable setup will probably appear on tomorrow night's charts. She can miss one day of trading since it does not COST her anything, and it is far better to sit back and wait for those high probability setups than it is to jump in when the odds are not heavily slanted in her favor, and her risk of losing the trade (and a substantial amount of money) is greater.

And that is the sum of Mrs. Watanabe's Secret: trade only when the odds are heavily in your favor using a method that is designed to identify those particular times and trades; use a semi-aggressive form of money management to take full advantage of the power of compounding; and use a long and duplicable series of small gains to grow her account into 7 figures in less than a year.

∧∧∧∧∧∧∧∧∧∧∧∧∧∧∧∧∧∧∧∧∧∧∧∧∧

If you've made it this far, you should be feeling at least a little bit excited about the idea that you too could become a "Mrs. Watanabe" yourself. After all, she has no formal training in any kind of investing, she has only a limited amount of time each day to devote to her trades, and she started out with a fairly small amount of money with which to fund her account.

That same description probably fits you like a glove.

Mrs. Watanabe's Secret
Part Four

Distinguishing Between Strong Signals versus Weak Signals When Trading "Mrs. Watanabe's Secret"

After learning the details of Mrs. Watanabe's Secret, several people in my Trade Room were asking for a more detailed explanation of how to spot Strong Trade Signals when using Mrs. Watanabe's trading method, and further, asked me to show some examples of Weak Signals.

In response to those requests, I put together this small tutorial.

By way of refresher, remember that we use 3 indicators trading Mrs.W.: Slope Direction Line (with settings at 34,2,0), the OsMA (using the factory settings), and the SignalAM (again, using the factory settings).

We are looking for all three indicators to give us the same signal (Buy or Sell) before we get into a trade.

Unfortunately, trading between 9:30 a.m. and 11:00 a.m. eastern time, we usually only see one "perfect" signal every 10 trading days or thereabout.

A "perfect" signal would be when all three indicators are all just starting to give the same signal, and at the same time. Here is a chart that demonstrates the "perfect" signal:

Plc 10-2

Here you'll notice at 22:40 the Slope had changed to Lime Green, the SignalAM was giving Buy signals (blue "x"'s) and the OsMA moved strongly UP above the "0" line. It took about an hour but you saw +20, and this trade ended up moving up from 1.3965 to 1.4090 over the course of the next 5 hours.

The problem with this setup/signal is what I mentioned earlier…we only see it once every couple of weeks at 9:30 a.m. or shortly thereafter. That's not a problem for the lady who taught me this method; she trades 100 lots at a time, and when she wins a trade, she makes $20,000. It doesn't take too many $20,000 days to have a decent month trading, and because she has grown her account to such an impressive size, she can afford to pass on trading any signal that falls short of the "perfect" setup discussed above, and only trades those signals that fit the "perfect" description.

Unfortunately, most of us do not have that luxury, so we need to be able to make sense of the "lesser" setups/signals in order to focus in on the trades that have the highest probability of winning.

Strong vs. Weak Signals

Let me get this part out of the way first. **The SignalAM indicator does not give out anything except Strong Signals.** In fact, if the SignalAM is not telling you to Buy, you don't Buy. Conversely, if it is not telling you to Sell, you do not sell.

On my chart, Red "x"'s make up the Sell Signal on the SignalAM, and Blue "x"'s make up the Buy signal. There is no intermediate color that comes into play.

For the Slope Direction Line, you do get Strong vs. Weak signals. The Strong Signal is when the Slope Direction Line turns color and supports the direction of your trade. On my charts, I use Lime Green for Buys and Magenta for sells. So if I am looking to Buy and the Slope Direction Line is just now turning Lime Green, that is a Strong Signal.

Unfortunately (again) many times you get signals from the other two indicators telling you to Buy or Sell, and the Slope Direction Line is the wrong color to support that trade. Rather than wait for the Slope to change color, we instead accept a Weaker Signal from the Slope to justify entering the trade.

The Weaker Signal from the Slope Direction Line occurs when the current candle closes on the "trade side" of the Slope Direction line without causing the Slope to actually change color. In effect, we are treating the Slope line as if it were a Moving Average line, and when we see the break of the line and a close of the candle on the "trade side" (meaning in case of a Sell trade the candle closes Below the Slope line, and in the case of a Buy the candle closes Above the Slope line) we will accept this as a weaker yet valid signal to enter into the trade.

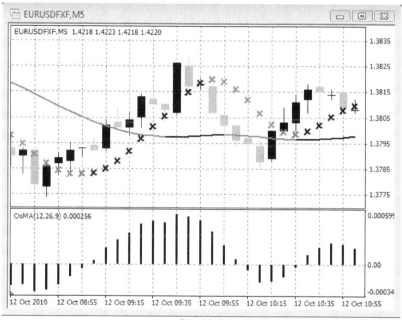

Pic 10-3

Here, the Slope has remained Magenta (meaning Sell) but at 9:15 a candle closed (barely) on the "Buy" side of the Slope (a Weak Buy Signal). The SignalAM gave a Buy signal at the same time, and the OsMA closed above the "0" line for the first time just one candle back, which is a Strong Buy signal. This would mean we had a Valid Buy Signal, and 30 minutes later we were out of the trade with +20 in profits.

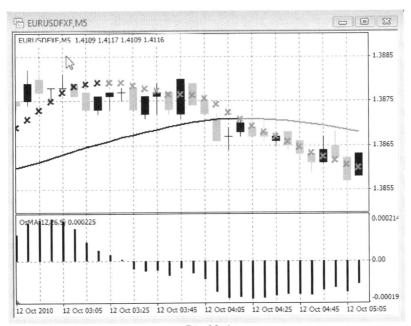

Pic 10-4

Here, the Slope Line is still Lime Green (meaning a Buy Signal) but the 4:10 candle closed on the Sell Side of the Slope Line (a Weak Sell Signal). The SignalAM had been giving off a Sell signal for several candles by that time, and the OsMA was also below the "0" line (and the current bar closed lower than the previous bar…a very strong Sell Signal). This was a valid Sell Signal at 1.3867 which hit +20 a couple of hours later (and ultimately bottomed out about 70 pips under our Sell price).

For the OsMA, the location of the bars in relation to the "0" line in the indicator tell you whether the signal you are getting from the OsMA is a Strong Signal or a Weak Signal.

Sensible Forex

If you are looking at the OsMA bars closing above the "0" line, and each bar is moving higher than the bar previous, you are getting a Strong Buy Signal. If the OsMA bars are closing below the "0" line and each bar is moving lower than the previous bar, it is a Strong Sell Signal.

Unfortunately (yet again) you are oftentimes faced with signals that don't meet these exact criteria. You are getting Buy signals from the other two indicators, but the OsMA is still below the "0" line, or you are getting Sell signals from the other two indicators, and the OsMA bars are still above the "0" line.

This is where the bar size in relation to the previous bar(s) comes into play. **If the other indicators are telling you to Buy, and the OsMA bars are still below the "0" line, but are moving upwards towards the "0" line, this is a weak but valid Buy Signal. If the other two indicators are giving you a Sell Signal, but the OsMA is still above the "0" line but is moving down towards the "0" line, this is a weak but valid Sell Signal.**

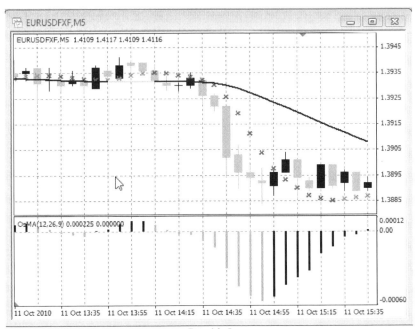

Pic 10-5

This isn't the best example I've ever seen, but it was the best one I could find today to demonstrate. At 14:15 the SignalAM turns red (A Sell Signal); the Slope turns Magenta (a Strong Sell Signal) but the OsMA is still above the "0" line, but the bar is shorter than the previous bar at 14:10, and moving towards a cross below the "0" line. This is a Valid Sell Signal (of course, with hindsight we can see a couple of candles later we have a more or less "perfect" setup at more or less the same price we got with a less than perfect setup. But we don't know what the future holds, and if we get a Less Than Perfect Yet Still Valid Signal, we take it. And in this case, we made an easy 20 pips within the 30 minutes after entering the trade.

213

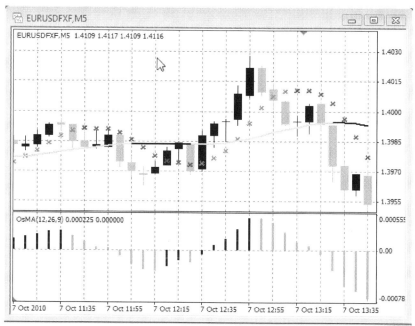

Pic 10-6

Same situation as the chart above, but going in the other direction. At 12:35 we had a Buy Signal from the SignalAM, and the Slope turned Lime Green at the same time (a Strong Buy Signal). The OsMA was still below the "0" line but was smaller than the previous bar and was moving towards crossing the "0" line and becoming a Strong Buy Signal. Instead of waiting,, we accept this as a Weak Buy Signal from the OsMA, and when combined with the strong Buy Signal from the Slope and the Buy Signal from the SignalAM, we have a Buy Trade at the close of the 12:55 candle. Assuming we got in right at the close, we bought at 1.3988 and made our 20 pips in less than 15 minutes.

Sensible Forex

Trading with Weaker Signals

This is the part where most people get confused; when are the weak signals strong enough to justify getting into a trade?

The rule I use is this: **you MUST have at least ONE STRONG SIGNAL** in addition to the SignalAM indicator before you can enter a trade.

What that means is this: The SignalAM is giving you a Buy or Sell Signal. Either the Slope Direction Line **MUST BE THE SAME COLOR** (meaning a Strong Signal) or the OsMA **MUST BE ON THE "TRADE SIDE" OF THE "0" LINE** in order to have a valid signal.

Additionally, the other indicator (the one NOT giving you a Strong Signal) **MUST BE GIVING YOU A WEAK SIGNAL** to take the trade.

So if the SignalAM is telling you to Sell, my Slope Direction Line **MUST** be Magenta if the OsMA is still above the "0" line (but moving down)...

OR...

If my SignalAM is telling me to Sell, the OsMA **MUST be BELOW** the "0" line if the color of the Slope Direction Line is still saying "buy" when the candle closes on the Sell side of the line.

In the case of a Buy Signal from the SignalAM, the Slope Direction Line **MUST** be Lime Green if the OsMA is below the "0" line (but moving up)...

OR

If my SignalAM is telling me to Buy, the OsMA **MUST** be above the "0" line and moving UP if the Slope Direction Line is still Magenta (but the current candle closes above the Slope line, of the Buy side).

WHEN NOT TO TRADE

Here is the most important part of this tutorial.

If the SignalAM is saying BUY, but the OsMA is still below the "0" line but moving up AND the Slope Direction Line is still Magenta but the current candle closes above the Slope Line (on the Buy Side of the Line) we **DO NOT HAVE A TRADE**.

In other words, if both the Slope Direction Line AND the OsMA are giving off Weak signals, **WE DO NOT TAKE THE TRADE**.

You want at least ONE of those two indicators to be giving off a Strong Signal before you put any money at risk.

The same rule applies in the case of a SignalAM Sell Signal: if the OsMA is still above the "0" line but moving down, and the Slope Direction Line is still Lime Green but the current candle closes below the Slope on the Sell Side of the line, you have two WEAK signals and you **DO NOT TAKE THE TRADE.**

Summary

SignalAM + Strong Signal + Strong Signal = TRADE

SignalAM + Strong Signal + Weak Signal = TRADE

SignalAM + Weak Signal + Weak Signal = NO TRADE

Appendix

To see all of the graphics from this book in living color…

To get free access to ALL of the indicators mentioned in this book…

To find listing and reviews of a handful of trading systems that just might be exactly what you need to start trading Forex profitably…

And to gain full and FREE access to a downloadable copy of my Trade Justification Form…

Visit **www.sensible-forex.com/buyerpage** and click on the appropriate links.

Sensible Forex

Sensible Forex

Made in the USA
San Bernardino, CA
21 January 2016